For Tami 7/14/14

9-1-1
WHAT IS YOUR EMERGENCY?

I hope you enjoy the book.

Best Wishes

Lucia #160

9-1-1
WHAT IS YOUR EMERGENCY?

**ACTUAL CALLS RECEIVED BY A 9-1-1 DISPATCHER
and insight into a dispatcher's life**

THE FUNNY, THE SAD AND THE UGLY

Lucia - Retired Dispatcher #160

authorHOUSE®

AuthorHouse™ LLC
1663 Liberty Drive
Bloomington, IN 47403
www.authorhouse.com
Phone: 1-800-839-8640

Published by AuthorHouse   12/05/2013

ISBN: 978-1-4918-3668-2 (sc)
ISBN: 978-1-4918-3667-5 (hc)
ISBN: 978-1-4918-3666-8 (e)

Library of Congress Control Number: 2013920974

TABLE OF CONTENTS

CHAPTER ONE

A TYPICAL HOUR IN A DISPATCHER'S SHIFT

During a typical hour, a dispatcher needs to be ready to take care of any type of emergency or non-emergency call. He/she needs to be able to adjust from a stressful emergency where your adrenaline is pumping to the next call of seemingly little importance. Calls come in back to back, and back and forth between emergencies and non emergencies. The following is a brief example of a typical hour answering the phones in Communications.

6:00 A.M.

Dispatcher: San Diego 911, dispatcher 160, what is your emergency?

Caller: I just stabbed my wife . . . .

—~m~—

6:20 A.M.

Dispatcher: San Diego Police, dispatcher 160, what are you reporting?

Caller: My neighbor's dog keeps crapping on my lawn; I need you to come out now.

6:23 A.M.

Dispatcher: San Diego 911, dispatcher 160, what is your emergency?

Caller: I have a shotgun in my hand, and want to end it all; I don't want to live anymore.

6:40 A.M.

Dispatcher: San Diego 911, dispatcher 160, what is your emergency?

Caller: I think I'm having a heart attack.

—ɯɯ—

6:42 A.M.

Dispatcher: San Diego Police, dispatcher 160, what are you reporting?

Caller: Some asshole parked his car blocking my driveway. I need to go to my palates class. Please send an officer as soon as you can.

—ɯɯ—

6:44 A.M.

Dispatcher: San Diego 911, what is your emergency?

Caller: This is a teller at Bank of America, we just got robbed.

—ɯ—

6:58 A.M

Dispatcher: San Diego Police, dispatcher 160

Caller: The idiot next door has been banging on his drums for the past four hours. I need a cop out here to make him stop.

CHAPTER TWO

GENERAL CALLS

The following are some general calls that came into San Diego Police Communications.

—〰—

Dispatcher   San Diego Police, dispatcher 160, how can I help you?

Male caller   I found a citation that was issued to my wife.

The charge on the citation is 647(b) of the California Penal Code.

I was wondering if you could tell me what that charge means.

The dispatcher paused a moment, hesitating to tell the unsuspecting husband that the charge 647(b) is for '**solicitation of prostitution**'. The dispatcher reluctantly gave the unsuspecting husband the bad news.

Dispatcher: The charge is 'solicitation of prostitution" sir, I'm sorry.

There was a long uncomfortable pause . . . finally the enlightened husband responded . . .

<u>Enlightened Husband:</u> Oh, I'll bet that explains the **fur coat** and **big screen TV** she told me she bought with the money she saved using **coupons.**

~~~~∿∿~~~~

A woman called 911 yelling obscenities. She was upset that another female was at her house refusing to leave. The irate woman demanded an officer come out and take the female to jail. The dispatcher began asking for a physical description of the woman.

<u>Dispatcher</u>   What race is she?

<u>Caller</u>   **She's a 'ho"!!**

<u>Dispatcher</u>   No, what **race** is she?

<u>Caller:</u>   **SHE'S A HO**!

The dispatcher continued, being just as persistent . . . .

<u>Dispatcher:</u> Well, she wasn't a **ho** when she was born . . . . What **race** is she?

The woman finally calmed down enough to give the dispatcher the information needed. Officers were dispatched to diffuse the argument and the woman was sent on her way.

———∿∿∿———

Dispatcher   911, what is your emergency?

Witness   I see a transient in a blanket. From the movement under the blanket, he is either **masturbating** or having a **seizure.**

Officers went out . . . . he was not having a seizure.

———∿∿∿———

A man called in to report a guy walking around outside, completely naked and dancing in the street.

The dispatcher began asking for the person's description . . .

Dispatcher: Is he White, Black, or Hispanic?

Caller: He's a white guy . . .

Dispatcher: How old does he look?"

Caller: I don't know man . . . I was looking at his **ass**, not his **face!**

Officers went out, contacted the naked 'light-on-his-feet' gentleman and transported him to County Mental Health for a 72 hour evaluation.

—⁓w⁓—

We received a 911 call from inside a house.

The dispatcher answered, "San Diego Police 911", and the line then disconnected.

We treat every 911 hang up as an unknown emergency.

When a 911 call comes into Communications, the house address and phone number are displayed on the dispatcher's screen. The dispatcher immediately typed up the limited information for an officer to respond to that address.

Then the dispatcher followed protocol and made a callback to the house to see if she could get more information. The callback was answered.

Dispatcher: Hello, this is the San Diego Police Department. We received a 911 hang up from your house. We have officers on the way. Is there an emergency there?

Embarrassed Caller: I'm so sorry. There is no emergency here. I came home from work and hit "redial" on my house

7

phone. I do this every night to check the last phone number that my husband dialed to see if a woman answers.

Evidently her husband knew she does this and decided to play a joke on her. The suspicious/embarrassed wife said, "He really got me good this time".

The dispatcher thanked the wife for answering and cancelled the officer's response.

—⟋⟋⟋—

A woman called in to report an unconscious man lying down on a bus bench.

The dispatcher got officers started and continued getting information.

The dispatcher initially thought the caller was being a Good Samaritan and concerned that this young man was hurt or having some type of medical emergency.

Well, not so much . . . . She was upset because there was no place for her to sit on the bus bench, so she "**kicked** him in the back" to see if he would wake up.

Officers and paramedics got out there, contacted him, and found him to be okay. He had just been drinking and fell asleep.

Sleeping beauty then got up and walked off, and the woman got her seat on the bus bench.

A man called asking for officers to go out to his girlfriend's house and make sure she was okay. He said he was out of town and could not go himself.

He explained he hadn't heard from her for several days, and she was not answering her phone. He was very worried about her.

Officers responded to the girlfriend's house to check her welfare.

When they got there, officers found her at the house with another man. It was apparent the officers interrupted them having sex.

The girlfriend calmly told officers that as soon as she was done, she would call her boyfriend.

The officers told her to have a nice day, and cancelled the call.

Officers often deal with situations involving persons threatening to kill themselves. Safety of the person threatening to kill himself, the officers themselves and the public is of utmost priority on all suicide calls.

Officers receive some crisis intervention training, but no call is exactly the same . . . .

We received a 911 call of a man threatening to jump off of a 4th story balcony.

He had a fight with his girlfriend earlier and made threats to kill her.

He is now on the balcony. His girlfriend and another friend are talking to him, trying to keep him from jumping.

The officers rushed out and were able to talk him down and back inside the apartment to safety. The distraught man was extremely upset.

After officers got the man to safety, they learned the reason the man tried to end his life.

He had just found out his girlfriend for the past two months was a **man**.

Officers transported him to a hospital facility for the night for everyone's safety.

(Could this have been a real U.F.O? We couldn't explain this one)

In January 1996, we received the following call:

<u>Dispatcher</u>   911 what is your emergency?

<u>Witness</u>   I have been seeing a blue, red, and white object in the sky. It has moved left and right. It's now over the 32nd St. Navy Base.

Two units in the area were seeing it too. The officers had a visual of something hovering, flashing red, white and blue.

We notified the naval base and asked if they had any helicopters or special assignments that could explain it.

They advised they did not know anything about it, but would check further and get back to us.

One of the officers witnessing this said the object was now over Coronado or possibly further out to sea.

Suddenly, a second object appeared over Pt Loma. The officer said the second object might be a helicopter.

When the officer looked at the object through binoculars, he thought it could be a satellite, but it had red,white and blue colors.

We never found out what it actually was.

All convicted sex offenders need to register in the State of California. A man called in with the following question:

> A long time ago, I was charged with attempted rape. All I did was **chase** her around the room. Do I still need to register?'

I referred him to our Sex Registrant's Unit. I would think there was probably a bit more to the story this guy left out.

A frantic male called in saying that his **penis** was **numb**, and asked if that meant he was having a **stroke**.

The police dispatcher transferred the call to the paramedics, and they responded to assist the caller.

Dispatcher: San Diego Police, dispatcher 160, what are you reporting?

Worried wife: My husband has not returned home from work. He is several hours late.

He works at a construction company and I am afraid something might have happened to him on the job site.

Can you go by and see if his white pickup is in the parking lot?

I am not able to go by and check myself.

Officers went out to the husband's job site and located him there.

He was fine, **but he was not alone.**

He told the officers he would call his wife and let her know he was okay.

He added, "**Please don't tell my wife about the dancing girls.**"

A woman called in to report her husband missing. Half way into the conversation, she changed her priority.

Dispatcher   San Diego Police, how can I help you?

Caller   I want to report my husband missing.

Well . . . Actually, I really need my <u>car</u>, and he's driving it.

How long will it take to get the stolen vehicle report in the system?

Dispatcher: Sorry, ma'am, we can not take a Missing Person's Report if he is voluntarily missing.

If he is driving your car, the car is community property. Therefore, no stolen report can be taken.

She was not happy about that, and hung up.

A woman called that her friend was out of control and had a violent seizure.

She also broke furniture in the apartment.

Her friend believes someone put a curse on her family and that she is now possessed.

Seven men are now trying to restrain her, but they cannot hold her down much longer.

They are asking for the police to get there fast.

Officers and paramedics rushed over and transported her to a hospital.

A woman called from Los Angeles and said she had a premonition that the house she owned in San Diego was being broken into.

She asked us to go out and check it for her.

The dispatcher politely said,

"Sorry, we don't do premonitions."

———〰———

A mother called from back East.

She said she had a premonition that her son was hurt.

The distressed mom asked if we could go out to his house and make sure he was okay.

We went ahead and sent officers out to check on him. He was fine.

The dispatcher called the mother back and put her mind at ease.

———〰———

It was about 5:00 in the evening when a 13 year old boy called 911, crying.

He said he had been kidnapped, tied up and held at gunpoint for an hour. He said this happened about 8:30 in the morning.

The boy went on to say, every time he tried to get away, the suspects pulled him back and threatened him.

Officers went out and were on scene with the young victim for an hour and a half.

He ended up admitting that he lied about the whole kidnapping incident. He had skipped school that day, and was afraid he would get in trouble with his parents. So he came up with that elaborate story.

Officers left, no report was taken. They had the parents and son work through it themselves.

—⁓⁓⁓—

Dispatcher: San Diego Police, dispatcher 160, what are you reporting?

Patient caller: I am a visitor from out of town and staying at a beach house in Mission Beach.

There is a guy that has been playing bongos all day on the boardwalk in front of my place.

As much as I like drums and bongos, I think 5 1/2 hours of it pounding in my head is long enough. Can you send a cop out?

Officers eventually went out on the noise complaint and asked the musician to take a rest or move down the boardwalk.

———〰———

Dispatcher: San Diego Police, how can I help you?

Caller: My neighbor has been playing the same song over and over for the past three hours. I love Abba, but hearing "Dancing Queen" non-stop is driving me nuts.

———〰———

Dispatcher: 911, what is your emergency?

Caller: I am the owner of an Inn.

We have been trying to have a tenant evicted for some time.

The guy is in his room now.

> In an attempt to deter the eviction, he told us he tied the drape cord around his testicles. So if anyone opens the door to get him out, they will cause him great injury.
>
> I can see the drape cord sticking out of his front door.

Officers got out to the Inn, thinking they were going to be facing a difficult call. But when they arrived, they found the tenant was fine. There was no cord wrapped around his testicles. He subsequently agreed to go ahead and check out of the Inn.

―――⌇⌇⌇―――

(You got to give this guy credit for finally getting his act together . . .)

A guy who had been arrested for drugs had completed his sentence and rehab.

He called his wife to pick him up from the facility. When she got there, he could see she was high on crack.

Evidently those rehab classes sunk in, because when he got home, he realized he no longer wanted to be in that type of environment.

So he called police and asked if officers could meet him outside their home. He wanted the officers to stand by while he picked up his belongings and told his wife he was leaving her.

Police responded to assist him.

—⟋⟋⟋⟍—

We received a call from a woman who was hearing a female neighbor screaming from inside a house down the street.

The caller was afraid the woman was being attacked or was in some type of trouble.

Officers went out and concluded the woman was 'practicing **scream therapy**'.

—⟋⟋⟋⟍—

A dispatcher saw an article in a San Diego newspaper and decided to share it with the other dispatchers:

> A male traveling through from New Mexico to Arizona ended up in Ocean Beach, (San Diego, California) at the end of I-8 with a map in his hand.
>
> He had a perplexed look on his face as to how he missed Arizona.

From time to time, citizens will call in to report seeing a suspicious package. They usually think it could be a bomb and are genuinely concerned. We take these types of calls seriously, and handle them as potential bomb calls. Often they turn out to be something other than a bomb. Once in a while it is . . . . Here are examples:

Sometimes it isn't . . . .

> An elderly woman called 911 when she saw a suspicious small blue plastic bag on her front driveway. She was afraid it was a bomb.

> Officers rushed out there and found the bag.

> It turned out that the woman's neighbor had gone fishing and left his bag of **fish bait** on the driveway.

> Officers removed the smelly fish bait and went on to the next call.

Sometimes it is . . . .

A woman called to say she found two sticks of dynamite with wires coming from it on the ground.

She picked it up and called police.

When officers got out there, they called for the bomb squad.

It was a some type of incenery device and had to be detonated.

(I've got to wonder, what was she thinking?!! If anyone ever sees anything like that . . . do not . . . do not . . . pick it up please!)

———〰———

More and more grandparents have had to take on the role of parenting because the real parents are both either working full time or in jail. It's difficult enough to have to take on this new role at a time when they should be relaxing and enjoying their later years. It's even sadder when the kids are out of control . . .

A frustrated grandmother called police. Her 12 year old grandson refused to change his baggy pants, and tuck in his shirt. The defiant grandson told his grandmother,

> 'You can't do anything to me, and I don't care if you call '**the law**'!

———〰———

Dispatcher: San Diego Police, what are you reporting?

Caller: A guy was exposing himself as I walked by his car. He was sitting in the passenger seat.

Dispatcher: What race was he? How old did he look?

Caller: I don't know, all I remember is his penis.

—⁓〰⁓—

A young teen called 911. He said two other boys were at his house saying they had information about two dead bodies buried nearby.

The boys said they found blood on a tree and possible pieces of brain. They were very upset and anxious to show officers where the blood, brains, and dead bodies were.

Officers responded to the teen's home. The two boys directed the officers to the spot they saw the blood and brain matter.

The boys' imagination got the better of them. What they saw was not blood and brain. There were no dead bodies either.

Officers gave the boys a ride home and went on to the next call.

—⁓〰⁓—

A man who drives a garbage truck called in.

As he emptied a dumpster into his truck, he heard voices coming from the dumpster. He thought transients might be inside it.

He called us and asked if officers could check his truck.

When they got out, sure enough, they did find a person inside the truck among the garbage. The poor man was frightened, but not injured.

CHAPTER THREE

GALLOWS HUMOR

Those in stressful occupations such as police and medical professionals may use a dark sense of humor as a coping mechanism.

This has been described as gallows Humor. Gallows Humor may sound offensive or unprofessional to others, but it can put some distance between themselves and the grim realities of their jobs, the unique working conditions and demands of their professions.

Some people may not understand why or how we can make light of some situations. If however, you can approach this book with an open mind, it may give you insight to how we cope through our shift.

Again, keep in mind, we always handled each call to the best of our abilities, and always gave each caller the professional respect they deserved.

The following calls in this chapter include thoughts or comments made by officers or dispatchers after the completion of the incident. Goofy or not, it helped us stay positive and would break up a normal stressful day.

—〜〜〜—

San Diego Police Officers responded to what initially came in as a car accident near the Wild Animal Park.

When the officers got there, they were shocked to see a deceased man inside the vehicle with a gunshot wound.

The car was right on the border of San Diego City's jurisdiction and the San Diego Sheriff's jurisdiction.

This posed a perplexing problem because the agency that would be assigned the homicide is determined by the location where the victim was found.

The dispatcher still had not confirmed with the officers exactly which side of the border of jurisdiction the car was. So the dispatcher asked the officer if the victim was shot in San Diego's or the Sheriff's area.

The officer replied, "I don't know . . . he's not talking . . ."

―――∿∿―――

Dispatcher: San Diego Police, how can I help you?

Witness: There are about 15 men and 7 women loitering on the corner.

They are all together, talking like they are in a meeting. And they are flagging down cars.

> This is a known prostitution corner. I think they are **pimps** and **prostitutes.**

(Perhaps it's a Pimp and Ho convention)

A guy called in. He said he is an alcoholic who drank too much, and now his head is going numb.

Paramedics responded to handle the call.

(Is that what they call a 'numb skull?")

A man called in to make a theft report. He said he drove his **wife's** car down to Tijuana to visit his **girlfriend**.

While he was there, the car was broken in to and a large amount of his wife's money was taken from inside the car.

(I wonder how he's going to explain that one to his wife.)

A man called 911. He was hearing a neighbor outside, cussing and yelling. He did not know why the guy was yelling. He thought people were fighting and asked if cops could go out.

Officers responded to see what the problem was.

It turns out the neighbor had been barbecuing chicken for a party.

He started cussing after he dropped a chicken, slipped on it, and fell to the ground.

(In true cartoon fashion . . . Can you picture this happening in a cartoon? The guy doing a quadruple flip, in a puff of smoke, and his head sticking out of the smoke?)

A **pastor** called from a **church**. He was reporting a car that had been parked in his church parking lot for a while. He did not know who the car belonged to and was concerned it might be stolen.

Dispatcher: How long has the car been parked there?

Pastor: **Four days** and **four nights**.

(I'm glad he didn't say forty days and forty nights!!)

A man called for a police report.

He said he had just gone into a taco shop to get something to eat. He started walking down the street, eating his burrito when a prostitute approached him.

She propositioned him and he ignored her.

This didn't set well with her. She got hostile, started arguing with him and grabbed his private parts.

The dispatcher told him officers would come out and take a report on the sexual assault.

She asked him for a description of the prostitute.

He gave the following . . .

Hispanic female, 5'6, medium build, wearing a dark tee shirt, jeans, and has a **BIG BUTT.**

(I can just hear the guy in court when the judge asks him if he can identify the suspect . . . Your honor, can the suspect please stand up and turn around?)

We received a call from a woman who had seen numerous scratches on a neighbor child. She felt the mother was physically abusing the child.

Police responded quickly to evaluate for possible child abuse.

The officers that responded eventually determined the child had been scratched by the family cat and there was no evidence of abuse.

(When the officers were leaving, they advised the dispatcher that the mother was pregnant and due today, so we might get more calls about screaming if she goes into labor.)

A witness called in a hit and run accident.

He saw the driver crash into the rear of a building, and then take off on foot.

The witness gave good information, and a detailed description.

Officers were dispatched and searched the area.

The suspect was soon apprehended a few blocks away.

He was talking on a payphone when the cops pulled up to him.

The officers soon determined that the suspect was drunk.

The irony of it all . . . .

It turns out he had just left an **A.A. (Alcoholics Anonymous)** meeting.

(He probably didn't like the bad coffee and stale donuts they were serving and opted for an alternative.)

(And who was he calling on the payphone, his sponsor? I think he should have thought about calling him sooner, don't you think?)

A woman called to report a nude man, masturbating in front of a window inside an apartment.

She also said the guy had some kind of a bright "spotlight" on himself.

(When officers arrived, they said they were able to take evidence pictures with their camera, and no flash was needed.)

One day, we received a call of an egg truck that overturned and dumped a partial load in the streets . . . .

(Omelets anyone?)

And if the truck flipped over, would the eggs be sunny side up?)

A woman called in. She was walking her dog down the sidewalk near her house.

As she walked by a tree, a man holding a black plastic bag jumped out and leaped towards her. He stopped, looked at her without saying anything, and then ran off.

She described him as follows;

A white male, in his 50's, 6 foot, with gray hair slicked back, wearing a **superman costume and a cape.**

There had been numerous complaints about this same guy in the past. He is usually sighted about 6:00 in the morning.

Officers and air support were dispatched.

He eluded capture. The officers asked neighbors to call if they see him again.

(Once again, he was faster than a speeding bullet.)

A call came in reporting a bicycle accident.

Officers arrived and contacted the bicyclist who was a 61 year old Greenbay Packers fan.

He told officers he always wore a helmet, but not today. Today he was wearing a "cheese head" hat because the Packers were playing.

Unfortunately, he had to brake fast. He went over the handlebars and landed, (you guessed it) on his head. He was shaken up, but was going to be ok.

(The moral of the story . . . it's a Gouda idea to always wear your helmet, so you don't cut the cheese.)

———

Dispatcher: San Diego Police, what are you reporting?

Caller: I manage a hotel here downtown.

A tenant of mine had been sunbathing on his balcony earlier.

Now he is by the front desk, completely naked. He oiled his body and is trying to swim across the lobby.

Officers went out to the hotel and contacted the tenant.

(He probably should have paid a little more and gotten a hotel with a pool, don't ya think?)

———

An officer driving down the street was **flagged** down by a man who just discovered his car had been stolen. The guy was extremely angry and obnoxious.

(I wonder which finger he used to flag down the officer?!)

―――ᙡ――

Officers who were arresting a man for a DUI, (Driving under the Influence of drugs or alcohol) sent the following warning to other officers in the field.

> You might want to avoid eating at (such and such) restaurant for a while . . . . We just arrested the chef for drunk driving and he's not happy with us.

(I wonder what threat the suspect made to prompt that warning.)

―――ᙡ――

A man called in, said he was ready to buy a car from a friend, and wanted to know if there were any outstanding tickets against it before he bought the vehicle.

After running the license plate, it was learned that the car was in the system as stolen.

The dispatcher informed the prospective buyer. Officers were dispatched to impound the vehicle, and have a little chat with this guy's so-called friend.

(With friends like that, who needs enemies?)

A woman heard a knock on her door and looked through the peep hole before opening it. Through the peep hole, she saw a man, completely nude standing in her doorway.

She promptly called police. When officers arrived, the guy started running, and the chase was on.

After a short foot pursuit the officers were able to catch up with him and take him into custody.

(Maybe he should have at least worn running shoes.)

A clerk working in a convenience store called.

> This is Sam. I'm calling from the convenience store on El Cajon Boulevard. There's a woman, about 300 pounds, completely naked, sitting on the floor, refusing to leave.

He called back after several minutes, asking when officers were going to get there. He was upset because customers were not coming in the store and he was losing business.

(For those of us who remember the 60's and the 'sit in' protestors . . . this takes it to a whole new level.)

We got a call from a security guard at a bus company.

He had arrested a man for trespassing and handcuffed him to a chair.

When the security guard was not looking, the suspect ran off.

The problem was the guy was still handcuffed to the chair!!!

Officers went out, and did not have much of a problem finding the guy.

(Now, if this guy was thinking, he would have run to an outside café, used the chair to sit down at one of the tables, and then ordered a cappuccino to blend in, right?)

A caller asked for police because a man and woman were in her garden having sex. By the time the police came out, the couple had left.

(I wanted to tell her, have you thought of planting rose bushes?)

———❦———

Dispatcher: 911, what is your emergency?

Caller: Are you Black?

Dispatcher: I don't know why it matters, what is your emergency?

Caller: Are you Black? I want to talk to a Black dispatcher.

Dispatcher: No, I am White, now what is your emergency?

Caller: I don't want to talk to you; I want to talk to a Black Dispatcher with a Master's Degree. I have an AA degree and want to talk to someone with a higher education.

(Well . . . excuuuuuse me . . . !)

She refused to tell me what the emergency was, so I transferred her to another dispatcher. It turns out she had no emergency what-so-ever. She just wanted to rant and rave.

———❦———

A clerk from a convenience store called in. He saw four white males urinating behind the store. Officers came out, but the men had already left.

(Is that what you would call a 'pissing contest'?)

—⟋⟍⟋—

Dispatcher: San Diego Police, what are you reporting?

Caller: My neighbor is having a loud, drunken party. There are three guys from the party, in the middle of the street, stark naked, playing saxophones and drums.

Officers contacted the musicians and advised them to go inside.

(After a few drinks, they probably thought they were members of the music group, 'Bare Naked Ladies".)

—⟋⟍⟋—

The local School Police called for assistance.

The principal of an elementary school said two sets of parents had been in the school cafeteria.

The four of them started arguing and soon they were throwing food at each other. This was during lunchtime, with all the elementary students looking on.

The parents were now in the principal's office.

(Wow, that's wrong on so many levels . . . and I wonder how long their detention was . . .)

———✺———

A witness called to report a guy walking out of a church with his pant pockets bulging. She saw him walk inside the church a few minutes earlier, and did not notice the deep bulging.

The caller thought he might have taken a large amount of change from the donation box. Police went out, but were not able to locate him.

(That's okay, someday; he will have to answer to a higher source . . .)

———✺———

A woman called in very upset. There was a dumpster behind her house in the alley.

She saw a man inside the dumpster going through the trash. He was scattering stuff all around and making a mess.

He had a shopping cart next to the dumpster . . . .

(Just browsing?)

———✺———

A pastor called in on the non emergency line many times one day regarding the same problem.

He kept asking for the same dispatcher each time. Despite the fact that the dispatcher handled the problem, he continued to call.

Finally, very frustrated with the caller, the dispatcher sent the following message around to all the other dispatchers . . . .

'The next time this pastor calls in asking for me, please tell him that I am on a break.'

(I sent a message back to her saying "Are you kidding? Lie to a pastor? I don't think so!!")

A woman claimed someone broke into her house and stole walnuts, cat food and money.

She wanted officers to come out and take a report. We did go out to evaluate the call.

(Hey, maybe the crook had a cat.)

A robber went into a taco shop and held up the employees.

Along with money, he took 15 burritos.

Officers found him walking down the street. They confiscated the money and burritos and then arrested him.

(I wonder how they are going to impound those burritos as evidence. And what will they call him in court . . . The burrito bandit?)

A husband arrived home from work and was met at the door by his wife holding a large butcher knife, threatening to stab him.

He called 911, and we rushed over.

It turns out his wife went to a **fortune teller** to get her fortune read.

The fortune teller told her that her husband was having an affair with a neighbor.

Officers went out and arrested the wife.

(A good fortune teller would have seen that coming.)

We received a call the day after Christmas from a parent with a very unhappy 11 year old son.

The father bought the very last Nintendo 64 game at the store.

The package was still sealed.

When his son opened the package there was a rock inside instead of a video game. The rock had been shaved down to the correct weight of the game system.

(The poor kid probably thought he was a bad boy and Santa played a trick on him . . . bah hum bug, what scrooge would do that?)

Can you imagine the joy the father had when he got the very last, extremely high demand Nintendo game on the shelf? And, you can imagine how happy his son was when he unwrapped his Christmas present and saw it was a Ninentendo 64.

And then the dream killer happened . . .)

A husband called 911. His wife was hysterical.

She had bought a box of hair coloring at the store. Evidently, someone had switched the blond color

tube with a black color tube, and now her hair was

jet black instead of platinum blond.

(Oh well, the good news is . . . it will wash away in 12-14 washes.)

―――~m~―――

A woman called 911 to report a boy, about 3 years old had been walking down the middle of the street.

The child was wearing a t-shirt, pants, and what looked like his mother's tennis shoes.

The caller took the child out of the street and said she would wait with the child until officers got there.

Officers rushed over and were able to find out where the boy lived.

As they walked the child to the door, they anticipated contacting a neglectful mother.

But instead, the mother was very distraught, and at a complete loss on what to do about the problem.

She explained her son had done this several times before. She was so desperate, that she put a couch, and a table in front of the door to keep her son inside the apartment.

The 3 yr old managed to move the **couch**, the **table** and unlock **three locks** to open the door and get out of the apartment!!

(Gees. Sign this kid up for the Iron Man competition . . . and let James Bond know his son is alive and well, and living in San Diego!)

An employee of a fast food restaurant arrived at work and noticed a Volkswagen was parked in the drive thru, and two guys were passed out inside the car.

Police and paramedics responded.

The men were arrested for being drunk.

(It was not a result of slow service . . . and that's going to end up being an expensive burger by the time they are done with court costs and lawyers.)

A call came in near a local high school. The citizen was reporting several drunken teens running around the streets naked.

(That reminds me of a day back when 'streaking' was the rage. I was driving by San Diego State University and saw a naked guy in a Roman Chariot being carried by several Roman Gladiators across the street. It was quite a sight. I guess some things never change.)

A woman called in regarding an on-going noise problem . . . .

She complained that an ice cream truck drives up and down the street every day playing "Turkey in the Straw" **over,** and **over,** and **over** . . . . and **over** . . . .

(I think you can empathize with her if you stop and hum a few bars of the song . . . over and over and over . . .)

A woman called, to report a **naked** man at her front door. When the dispatcher asked her for a description of the suspect, she said his name was "**Joe**".

(I wonder how she knew his name was Joe. Obviously, he was not wearing a name tag!!)

A very angry man called, wanted to file a battery report. He claimed someone hit him with a **bean burrito**.

Officers went out to evaluate the call. He was not injured by the burrito, and the officer did not take a report.

(242 CA. P.C. is the penal code for battery . . .

I've seen 242/fist . . . 242/frying pan . . . 242/ stick . . .

But 242/burrito? Seriously . . . ?)

—⚬⚬—

A guy robbed a business wearing a Richard Nixon mask.

The dispatcher made the following comment:

(I can just picture it . . . the guy running down the street, shaking his head, and with both hands in the air, and four fingers up, yelling . . . I am not a crook, I am not a crook.)

—⚬⚬—

Our police helicopter, ABLE (Airborne Law Enforcement) will often assist officers on the ground. Neighbors sometimes call in complaining about the loud noise of the helicopter. But a woman called in with a different complaint. ABLE was looking for a suspect when the woman called in . . .

Caller: The police helicopter keeps circling my neighborhood.

            My friend and I are sunbathing. I am wondering if they are doing that to look at us.

(Oh, please. I guess they think officers have a lot of time on their hands . . .)

—⁓—

A jilted lover called from another state.

She was very upset because her fiancée proposed to her on Christmas and then split to San Diego. She wanted us to find him for her.

The dispatcher advised her we cannot look for an adult who is voluntarily missing . . .

(I'll bet she wishes she had gotten him a GPS tracker for Christmas.)

—⁓—

Dispatcher: SD 911, what is your emergency?

High Caller: I was smoking crack with this girl. We started fighting, so I want her out of here.

(The caller said this so matter-of-fact, with no hesitation, as if they were having . . . "tea, crack and crumpets" . . .)

—ᛞᛢᛚ—

We received a call from a customer inside K-Mart.

The store was having a mega sale.

Two die-hard shoppers were inside the store having a drag out, knock down fight. They were throwing each other to the floor in the woman's underwear aisle.

They had been fighting over a piece of merchandise they both wanted.

One woman had a lot more merchandise in her cart than the other.

(Maybe she had better wheels on her cart and could move faster. So she was able to speed down the aisles, grab, and throw those deals in her cart, upsetting the other shopper.)

—ᛞᛢᛚ—

Dispatcher   911, what is your emergency?

Caller   I need the police to come out. I am afraid.

Dispatcher   Why are you afraid?

Caller   My neighbor told me 'Good Morning' and that frightened me.

The dispatcher advised her that we cannot send officers out there for a call like this unless there are threats made or more information to imply a threat.

(Gees . . .)

———〰〰〰———

Dispatcher: San Diego Police, how can I help you?

Caller: I recently had a "boob job".

                I also just bought $1,400 worth of clothes. My new clothes were still in my car.

                Yesterday, I drove to my boyfriend's house to break up with him, and found him with another woman.

                When I walked back to my car, I saw someone had broken into my car and stolen all my new clothes.

Today, I went to my girlfriend's house to tell her what happened, and to get some sympathy, and I found her wearing some of the clothes that were stolen from my car.

My girlfriend denies stealing my clothes. She claims she found the clothes lying on the sidewalk, and suggests a transient must have stolen them from my car.

(Wow, it sounds like this woman needs to get new friends and a new boyfriend to go along with that new boob job.)

Dispatcher: 911, what is your emergency?

Witness: I just witnessed a hit and run. The guy hit a neighbor's parked car and then took off.

The suspect is driving one of those rental moving trucks. Right now he is moving into a house down the block.

Officers went out and contacted the new neighbor.

(I'll bet the 'welcome wagon' won't be visiting him with a bundt cake and warm chocolate chip cookies.)

A man visiting from Idaho had been sleeping in the back seat of his car.

He woke up to find a suspect sitting in the driver's seat stealing his vehicle.

When the suspect realized the car owner was in the car, the suspect got out and ran off.

Officers came out for the report.

(I wonder who was more surprised, the car owner who woke up or the thief who didn't think any one was in the car and now realized that 'auto theft' charge just turned into a 'kidnapping' charge.)

A woman was arrested on a theft charge.

We ran her history and found **54** AKA's (also known as) . . . So she had gone by 54 different names . . .

(How does one person keep all those names straight??!!)

We got a call from a hair salon called . . . .

"Oooo Girl . . . . **who did your hair?"** . . . .

(Now that's a good name for a hair salon) . . .

An employee of the "Show offs Hair Salon" called to report a male exposing himself to the employees and customers.

(I guess he took the name of the business literally.)

A woman called to report vandalism. She said the guy next door caulked the open slats of her fence.

Officers went out. The accused neighbor admitted caulking the fence. He went on to explain why . . .

He was getting complaints from neighbors for gardening in the nude in his backyard.

(I'd say he did her a favor, don't you?)

A woman who lives near a church called in a noise complaint. She was upset that every Sunday, there was loud singing and yodeling coming from the church.

(Must be a Swiss church.)

—⁓〰⁓—

Dispatcher   San Diego Police, what are you reporting?

Caller   My cell phone and wallet were stolen off my work desk when I stepped out of the office.

To add insult to injury, the suspect used my cell phone to call my husband's cell phone. His number is programmed in my phone.

When my husband answered his cell phone the suspect said,

"Hi, my name is Dan, thank you for the phone."

(Wow, that's a pretty brazen crook, isn't it? or on the other hand, it's never too late to start using manners.)

—⁓〰⁓—

The manager of an apartment complex called to complain about two males who had set up a massage table at the pool area.

One was waxing the other's legs and massaging him inappropriately.

There were children nearby.

Officers went out.

(What were they thinking?!)

—⟋⟍⟋—

We received a call that a naked guy was standing at a bus stop on a very busy street. As women walked past him he would wave his pants in the air and smile.

Officers responded and arrested him.

(I would think if the women pointed and laughed as they walked by, he might have been humiliated enough to put his pants on and jump on the very next bus.)

—⟋⟍⟋—

A woman called because she and another woman had been fist fighting over a parking space in the zoo parking lot. The caller claimed she won the fight. She was still upset because after the fight, the other woman tore off a flag from the caller's car and put it on her own car, and then calmly walked into the zoo.

(Gees . . . all over a parking space . . . I thought the animals were supposed to be inside the zoo.)

—⟋⟍⟋—

A witness saw a guy who appeared to be under the influence of drugs.

He was on a dumpster, jumping up and down, barking like a dog, and trying to get onto a 2nd story ledge.

Officers were dispatched out there, but were unable to locate him.

(Maybe we should have checked the animal shelter.)

The woman's jail in San Diego is called Las Colinas Women's Facility.

A woman called us asking for the phone number to "Las Colinas **reservations**".

(Ha!! . . . I never thought anyone would consider jail as a vacation getaway spot, but again, I'm sure they have great rates.)

CHAPTER FOUR

LOVE, MARRIAGE AND DOMESTIC VIOLENCE
Or
LOVE IS FOREVER, UNTIL YOU CALL 911

273.5 P.C. is the California Penal Code for Domestic Violence.

(a) Any person who willfully inflicts harm upon a person who is his or her spouse, former spouse, cohabitant, former cohabitant, or the mother or father of his or her child, corporal injury resulting in a traumatic condition is guilty of a felony.

Law Enforcement is mandated by law to dispatch and evaluate each report of Domestic Violence, and to enforce any evidence of force or fear.

Domestic Violence calls make up a large portion of the calls that come into the Communications Division of the San Diego Police Department. Each call is taken seriously, and handled in a professional manner by the dispatcher, and the responding officers.

I also want to say, I never downplayed or made light of any D.V. call that I took.

Having said that, some of the calls are pretty funny. Here are some examples . . . .

Officers were dispatched to all of the following calls whether or not a crime had occurred to evaluate for any D.V. evidence.

—⁓〰⁓—

Dispatcher   San Diego 911 what is your emergency?

Caller   My wife is leaving to get her nails done, and I want her to stay home and cook dinner.

This husband was very serious, and thought he had a valid complaint.

—⁓〰⁓—

A frantic woman called to say her **boyfriend** was in her apartment refusing to leave.

She was very upset because her **husband** was going to be coming home soon.

She wanted the police to get her boyfriend out before her husband got there.

—⁓〰⁓—

Dispatcher   San Diego Police, how can I help you?

Caller   Can the police come out and make my husband take a bath or get out of bed?

Dispatcher   Sorry m'am, we can't legally force your husband to take a bath.

———ᄿᄿᄿ———

A woman called because a man she knew was in her house refusing to leave.

The dispatcher asked if the man was her boyfriend or ex-husband.

The woman replied matter-of-factly,

"No, he's just a sex partner. He already has a wife."

———ᄿᄿᄿ———

A woman called 911.

She said a man was trying to break in through the front door. She claimed she did not know who the person was.

She also claimed she was unable to give a description.

The dispatcher kept the woman on the line until officers arrived. During the call, the dispatcher could hear the doorbell ringing constantly and loud knocks at the door.

Officers rushed over.

It turned out; the would-be burglar was the woman's **husband**. And the woman was inside with her **boyfriend.**

———ɯ———

An angry husband called.

He wanted police to come out because his wife took the TV **remote control** and would not give it back to him.

He was upset because he had to get up to change the channels.

He told the dispatcher he is on probation and doesn't want to hit his wife, but he can't take it anymore.

Officers went out and calmed down the husband.

———ɯ———

Dispatcher   911, what is your emergency?

Caller   My wife is trying to attack me with a large knife. I was just upstairs with my **cousin Kathy**. I don't know why she wants to stab me.

While this dispatcher was on the line with the husband, another dispatcher received a call from the same address. It was his wife.

The wife went on to explain, Kathy, was **not his cousin.**

The wife arrived home early and caught the two of them in a very compromising situation.

Officers went out and though they sympathized with the wife, she was arrested for brandishing the knife.

———〰———

A woman called 911.

She and her estranged husband had been at a restaurant together having dinner.

They got into an argument and he took off in the car leaving her stranded.

She was very irate and demanded we track down her husband to get her boyfriend's things out of the car.

———〰———

Dispatcher: SD police, how can I help you?

Caller: I want you to come out. My boyfriend won't stop talking and he's keeping me up.

Please come and get him. He's making me sick.

A jealous husband called to report his wife was smoking crack with another man. He was very upset.

He was more than willing to give the dispatcher all the information she needed . . . . including that she always keeps the crack in her underwear.

(It's funny how secrets surface when you 'tick' off your other half.)

Dispatcher: San Diego 911, what is your emergency?

Caller: I want to report that my husband is committing Domestic violence.

Dispatcher: Okay, so what is he doing?

Caller: He is in **sales.**

Dispatcher . . . No, I mean **what is he doing to you now?!**

CHAPTER FIVE

5150/11550

The following codes are used for persons who are having psychiatric issues or are under the influence of drugs.

5150 W.I. (Welfare and Institution Code)

is a section of the California Welfare and Institutions Code which allows a qualified officer or clinician to involuntarily confine a person deemed to have a mental disorder that makes them a danger to him or her self, and/or others and/or gravely disabled.

11550 H.S. (Health and Safety Code)

(a) No person shall use, or be under the influence of any controlled substance . . . .

The calls in this chapter are from persons who are either under the influence of drugs or were having psychiatric issues.

I used the exact words that were used by the callers.

Therefore, their statements usually did not make sense and were irrational.

Also, any celebrity mentioned is the figment of their imagination. <u>No celebrity was ever involved in any way.</u>

Officers were dispatched to these calls if there was any indication the callers or any one else was in a danger.

Again, I want to emphasize that in no way did we treat any of these callers with disrespect or minimize the help that they needed. We handled each call professionally and without ridicule and got them the help they needed.

But let's face it, these calls are funny.

Read each call slowly, and then take a minute to think about the craziness that was going on inside their head when they called in.

Seriously, you can't make up this stuff . . . .

A woman called 911.

She wanted us to come out and check if she was **dead** or **alive**.

Another woman called . . . .

I was just in the bathroom, rinsing my dentures and all of a sudden the light in the living room went on. The switch was actually flipped on.

I know there is a ghost in this house.

I was wondering if you could give me the phone number to "**Ghostbusters**".

Do you know if they are **expensive** or not?

———

Dispatcher: San Diego Police, what is your emergency?

Caller: I would like to take a blood test to prove I'm not the **anti-Christ.**

(The dispatcher, who showed no reaction to the call, referred him to our lab unit where blood is drawn for D.U.I.'s, etc.)

Dispatcher Sir, we give blood tests on Tuesdays and Thursdays from 8:00 to noon. You'll have to call back then.

———

Dispatcher: 911, what is your emergency?

Caller: I am hallucinating, I'm really trippin' . . . I want to be transported to Jupiter.

Officers got out there and contacted him.

Then transported him to a hospital facility.

When an officer is going to transport someone, he will usually say, "11-48 (transporting) to County Mental Health.

This time the officer said, "**1148 to Jupiter**".

—⁓—

Dispatcher   911, what is your emergency?

Caller   I want paramedics . . . . I also want a pepperoni pizza with extra cheese.

Dispatcher   Why do you need paramedics?

Caller   A Chinese noodle is stuck in my thigh, the only one willing to sign my rights away are the injured.

—⁓—

Dispatcher   911, what is your emergency?

Caller   My girlfriend is bleeding; she just got dropped off by a U.F.O.

Officers rushed out. There was no U.F.O and no bleeding girlfriend.

A woman called claiming to have gotten involved with Kurt Kobane and Nirvana.

She said she is clairvoyant and gifted.

She went on rambling, said she is afraid of Courtney Love because she (Courtney) has nun chucks and studies martial arts.

The caller thinks Courtney is going to show up at her house.

Police arrived and transported her to a mental facility for evaluation.

Dispatcher   911, what is your emergency?

Caller   Moonfairy is being told by a higher source that I should hurt myself.

Officers responded and took her to a facility for 72 hour evaluation.

A woman called police several times to report break-in's to her home.

The first time she reported laxatives taken.

The second time she reported 3 cassette tapes stolen.

Officers went out and found no evidence of a break in to her home. She was not a danger to herself or anyone else, so they left and cancelled the call.

A man called 911 from County Mental Health . . . . Saying the following . . . .

> This is **James Bond**. I want to apologize to the Chief of Police for not writing to him for the past three days.

> But I am out doing undercover work as best I can.

> As soon as I uncover some crime in the city, the Chief will be hearing from me. . . . .

(With that, he hung up.)

A witness reported a naked man hiding in a stairwell near a busy intersection. Whenever a female driver stopped at the light, he would then jump out of the stairwell and pound on the car windows.

Officers located the guy and arrested him.

(I wonder how they were able to grab him and get those cuffs on.)

—⦿—

Dispatcher   911, what is your emergency

Caller   I am very upset.

My next door neighbor is deliberately causing extreme heat to come through our adjoining wall.

The heat is burning my skin.

I want you to arrest him.

I tried putting aluminum foil on the wall, but it's not helping.

We went out to make sure she was okay.

—⦿—

Dispatcher: San Diego 911, what is your emergency?

Caller: There is a guy harassing two teenage girls at a Trolley Stop.

Dispatcher: What is your name?

Caller: **Pablo Picasso, perhaps you have seen my paintings?**

Officers still went out to check if any teens were being harassed.

———⟋⟍⟍⟍⟋———

We received a call from a male . . .

Dispatcher... San Diego 911, what is your emergency?

Caller: Supervisor please . . . .

Dispatcher: What is this regarding?

Caller: Pickles . . . . pickles . . . . we have Officer Wade and we are holding him hostage.

If we don't get our pickles in 7 minutes, then we'll blow him away if things don't go our way.

So if you can, send the SWAT team to come over, we are tired of having the children go hungry.

Officers responded. There was no Officer Wade, and no one was being held hostage. We got the caller medical help.

(I hope they include pickles with his meals . . .)

———⟋⟍⟍⟍⟋———

A male called from County Mental Health.

Caller: I am Robocop, my devices are cramped. I have a **slug** in my neck and the nurses aren't helping me.

(Is it a slug? Or are his screws just loose?)

———〰️———

A woman called . . .

Caller A doctor cut a hole in my head.

Then he cut off my ear. When he sewed it back on, it's not even with my other ear.

He took the hearing out of my left ear.

I didn't know the hole was still there.

So he did another surgery that affected my left breast. I paid him $12,000.

———〰️———

Caller Rick Nelson is really alive. He just changed his name to Graham Nash and is singing country western now.

Richard (Rick Nelson) was going to marry me on New Years Eve, and the church was filled with people, but I didn't show up because I got kidnapped.

———ɷ———

A man who thinks he is Spiderman called in for police backup . . . .

Dispatcher   911 what is your emergency?

Caller   This is Spiderman, I need backup. Probably two black and whites should do it.

———ɷ———

A male called making unspecific threats against the police department. He had called several times that day.

He was upset that his cross bow was confiscated and in our property room for evidence.

He said he doesn't like female officers and threatened to carry out his threat, but would not elaborate.

The dispatcher kept him on the line until officers got out there.

During his conversation with the dispatcher, he kept asking for Axel Rose.

He claimed to work for George Bush, Frank Sinatra, the Catholic Church and the C.I.A.

On a previous call, he said his friend was being held hostage by the actor Michael J. Fox.

He had a history of drug use. Officers went out to calm him down.

After talking with the officers, he said he really didn't want to hurt anyone and promised not to make those threats again.

The officers then left.

(I'd say the officers impounding his cross-bow was a good call.)

—⟋⟍—

Dispatcher   San Diego Police, how can I help you?

Caller   I am calling from Brazil, I want to report something that happened in San Diego.

Mick Jagger and David Bowie were in my room doing sorcery. Mick Jagger and David Bowie tickled me until I had an orgasm. Jerry Hall has no internal organs. They are musicians in the church. They came back and used me to get my internal organs.

———∿∿∿———

This is so sweet . . . .

A man called 911 from inside County Mental Health; he was singing "Happy Birthday" to his mom.

The dispatcher called C.M.H. and asked a staff member to let him call his mom for the birthday wish.

———∿∿∿———

A woman called to say burglars are hypnotizing her, moving her slippers and unscrewing her cable TV.

———∿∿∿———

A man called, complaining that his neighbor is outside yelling, not making sense, and chanting words like a parrot.

———∿∿∿———

A woman called and claimed she was going out with Prince Charles.

———∿∿∿———

Caller: This is Bob Dylan the famous singer. Someone is trying to kill me.

            I just had these premonitions, and I am very frightened.

72

Officers were sent to get the gentleman the help he needed, it was not Bob Dylan.

—⟋⟍⟋—

A male called to say he figured out how to talk to the magnetic tape on his credit card.

The dispatcher asked if he figured out how to raise his credit limit.

We went out to make sure he was okay.

—⟋⟍⟋—

An employee from a fast food restaurant called . . .

He said a woman was inside, making a mess, throwing ketchup all over and yelling that Frank Sinatra is telling her to do it.

—⟋⟍⟋—

Dispatcher   911, what is your emergency?

Caller   I've got a problem here.

I have **imaginary** people hollering at my family.

Can you please send an **imaginary** police car to arrest them?

(Okay, with this call, you need to paint a visual picture as it unfolds to get the full effect . . .)

Officers patrolling the beach area drove up on a female who was clearly under the influence of drugs, possibly LSD or PCP. This was the way it played out until the officers were able to get her handcuffed. Try to picture it . . . .

As officers got to Sunset Cliffs Blvd. and Voltaire St., a female jumped out into the intersection.

She began dancing ballet . . .

Then she mooned the officers with her front and back side.

After that she jumped on the hood of the police car.

She then hopped on the light bar, performing more ballet.

Finally she gracefully leaped off the trunk of the police car and into the officer's arms.

The officers were finally able to handcuff her. They requested an ambulance to take her to the hospital. She was under the influence of some type of substance. One of the officers went in the ambulance with the ballerina to make sure she did not get violent with the E.M.T.'s. The other officer followed the ambulance in his police car.

———ɱ———

(Here is another call you should make a visual picture . . .)

Dispatcher 911, what is your emergency?

Caller Heat is coming up through my feet, acting as a magnet and moving me around the room.

(Think about it . . . a man moving around the room because of a magnet under the floor, it's like a cartoon . . . You can't make up this stuff!)

———ɱ———

A man called for police after a woman told him the following . . .

> The President would be killed and Raquel Welch needs to be notified so that she is appointed President immediately.

Officers responded and the Secret Service was notified. It is procedure to notify Secret Service any time there is a threat against the president. They responded to evaluated the woman and determine if it was a valid threat.

———ɱ———

Officers were going out to check the welfare of a man to evaluate him for possible mental crisis. As officers were enroute, the dispatcher continued to talk to him. This is to make sure we stay in contact with him in case the situation changes, and also so we don't lose contact with him. One of the first and most important questions a dispatcher will ask is if there are any weapons in their possession. Even though this caller was very co operative and passive, we still ask . . . .

Dispatcher: Mr. Smith, do you have any weapons with you?

Caller: 'No, but I have **three light bulbs**, a **bottle of Mountain Dew** and a ½ **gallon of ice cream**.'

Officers determined he was fine, thanked him and left for the next call.

Dispatcher 911, what is your emergency?

Caller Hi, this is John, the guy who hears voices. Tell the officers to stop yelling at me.

A concerned father called. He said his young kids were playing in the backyard and found a .22 pistol that someone must have ditched in the yard.

The father actually saw them playing with the gun.

A husband called because his wife was high on alcohol and crack cocaine.

She was out of control and being combative.

He said he just got out on a work furlough program and didn't want any problems, so he was calling us for help.

As the dispatcher was typing up the information for responding officers, she could hear the wife in the background ranting and raving, and yelling a 'mile a minute'.

At one point the wife picked up the extension phone and began yelling, "chemicals, chemicals in my face . . . burning!" . . .

The dispatcher was ready to get paramedics rolling when the wife realized there were no chemicals and said,

"Never mind, it's just **water**" . . . . And she hung up . . .

Officers went out and transported her to a hospital.

<u>Dispatcher...</u> 911 what is your emergency?

<u>Caller</u>　　　The Goodyear Blimp is flying in my direction and giving me nose bleeds in San Diego.

I am chemically sensitive . . . wait . . . . (he hesitated for a moment)

Now the blimp did a 90 degree, turned and went north instead of south and didn't follow me up the hill.

Never mind . . . .

And he hung up.

He was from a payphone. Officers went out to make sure he was okay, but were not able to locate him.

———ᵚᵚ———

<u>Dispatcher:</u> 911, what is your emergency?

<u>Caller:</u>　　　Someone has broken into my house; they always break in while I am sleeping.

The last time this happened they stole 75 cents, scratched a picture and munched on my tomato. I know I didn't eat it, because I slice them.

Dispatcher   911, what is your emergency?

Elderly caller My ex-landlord is spying on me with satellites and bugging my phone.

A guy called for police saying demons came out of the walls and floors of a vacant house.

Officers went out and contacted a group of young men at the vacant house.

They determined the demons coming out of the walls and floors were brought on by the narcotics the men had taken.

There was no evidence of foul play or danger to them. Officers subsequently returned all involved to their homes.

A woman called, saying there were midgets running around in her apartment surveying her, buzzing her ears, and burning her body.

Officers responded and transported her to our mental facility for evaluation.

Dispatcher   911, what is your emergency?

Caller   I found two rats and put them in a cage in my bathroom. It looks like an explosive device and "pull tabs" on the animals.

Officers went out . . . there were no rats, and no explosive device. Officers evaluated her and left.

———〰———

A 90 year old woman called to say her dead sister-in-law broke into her house.

———〰———

A man called 911 to say a couple of Vice Detectives were trying to feed him to a shark.

———〰———

A man called claiming "Life forces" and a female were inside his body that only a helicopter could spot.

———〰———

A woman called saying an F.B.I. agent was sleeping in her bed.

———〰———

A woman called 911 to say the Mafia was spiritually harassing her.

—◊◊◊—

Dispatcher   911, what is your emergency?

Adult caller   I need an ambulance,

I just swallowed a bug.

I just swallowed a cockroach and my parents won't take me to the hospital, **they're looney**.

My stomach is fluttering.

I'm Catholic and it's against everything I believe in.

(Is it Friday, and is the cockroach considered meat?)

It turns out she was having a reaction to her anxiety medication. She really didn't ingest anything.

—◊◊◊—

Dispatcher   San Diego 911, what is your emergency?

Caller   Hitler is alive and well and has a photo shop at the beach.

—◊◊◊—

Dispatcher   San Diego 911 what is your emergency?

Caller   Midgets and robots are breaking into my house and trying to burn down my house. They are tapping my phone and going up on my roof.

Dispatcher 911, what is your emergency?

Elderly caller A man is in my garage, crying, crying. He won't talk to me. I covered him with a blanket.

When officers got out there, the man in the garage turned out to be a large bag of dog food.

A male called in with slurred speech, possibly drunk.

Caller: I want to get paid for giving the world love. (He repeated this over and over.)

He was evaluated and transported to the psychiatric hospital.

Later, the dispatcher asked the Pert (Psychiatric Evaluation Response Team) if he was having a medical problem.

They felt he just had not taken his psychiatric medication.

The PERT Techs added . . . . he was trying to **swear at us**, but it was difficult **because he had no teeth.**

(And all the key swear words have s's in them.)

—⁓ﾟﾟ⁓—

Dispatcher: What is your emergency?

Caller   I'm being held hostage by the CIA via airwaves.

—⁓ﾟﾟ⁓—

Dispatcher   911, what is your emergency?

Caller   There are three midgets running around the house, holding onto strings with fire shooting from them.

It stings when it hits you.

They are here because Sheriff Roche lost the election, and they are here for retaliation.

—⁓ﾟﾟ⁓—

Dispatcher   911 what is your emergency?

Caller	There are midget officers flying small planes and landing on my phone lines to listen in to my conversations.

A woman repeatedly called 911, saying that her pet dog turns into Satin. She said his eyes get funny and his face changes.

A woman called to demand that we stop programming her software. She says she knows we are doing it, and it's getting into her brain.

Dispatcher	911 what is your emergency?
Caller	Homosexuals are trying to turn me into a robot.

Dispatcher	911, what is your emergency?
Caller	Martians are harassing me.

Dispatcher	911 what is your emergency?

Caller   The raindrops are telling me to do something bad. I don't want to hurt anyone or myself.

I want to go to the hospital. The drops are telling me what to do . . . . wait . . . .

(He keeps stopping to hear what the raindrops tell him.)

The raindrops are saying this is not a good time.

Dispatcher   Is your address . . .

The dispatcher gave the address that was displayed on the screen to the caller to verify his location . . . .

Caller   Yes, how did you know, can you hear them too?

At that point, the officers arrived on scene and contacted our caller.

After officers evaluated him, they relayed back to the dispatcher that everything was okay . . .

Normally, on a call, when officers determine the situation is stable, they will relay back to the dispatcher . . . . **Code 4.**

This time the officers relayed back . . . .

Code 4 with 'rain man'.

The officers then transported him to the hospital for evaluation.

A woman called that her 30 year old son had mental problems.

He was sleeping in the alley behind her house and refused to come inside.

She said he thinks he is a dog.

She told her son she wanted to take him to the hospital, but he was refusing to go with her.

The dispatcher told the mother to tell her son she would take him to the dog hospital.

She did, and that worked. The mother was able to get her son to the hospital for help.

A male called to report six people in a tree having sex.

He said the tree was in a vacant lot.

He went on to say he had a flashlight and would be standing by for the officers to direct them to the tree.

He called back several times, upset that officers were taking too long to get out there.

An officer who heard the call over the air advised he remembered this same guy called in a month earlier.

This same guy reported people having sex on the roof of a fast food restaurant.

On the prior call a month ago, officers met the man in front of the restaurant.

The man was still seeing the people on the roof, but there was no one there.

Nevertheless, the officers continued out to the new location.

Again, there was no vacant lot, no tree big enough to hold six people, and no one having sex.

———∽∽∽———

Dispatcher   911, what is your emergency?

Caller   My wife is in a wheelchair. She has been in the Witness Protection Program since she was 7 years old.

She witnessed the murder of her parents by the Mafia. Her twin sister is in on it.

Now I think my wife has been kidnapped because the person that came home tonight was not my wife.

She is pretending to be my wife.

I know she is not my wife because I saw this woman get up from the wheelchair and walk around.

I became sure it was not her when she put two left slippers on her feet.

———〰———

Dispatcher   911, what is your emergency?

Caller   I just want to let you know that Ronald Reagan and George Bush are killing people in Sierra Mesa.

They are putting them in boxes called crucifixes which are boxes with knives.

———〰———

Dispatcher 911, what is your emergency?

Caller   My apartment complex is being under surveillance. I want to know why.

There are blinking lights in the hallway secretly taking pictures of everyone going by. They are controlling lights from the outside.

When I call phone numbers from my phone I keep getting a recording saying the numbers are disconnected.

They are trying to make me think **I'm crazy.**

(News flash . . .)

———〰———

The following caller was a patient from County Mental Health . . . .

Dispatcher   911, what is your emergency

Caller   I'm John Lawso from the F.B.I. They're all looney in here and I don't have my gun.

———〰———

Dispatcher   911, what is your emergency?

In a Special Agent voice the caller replied . . . .

Caller   This is Special Agent Maytag, with the F.B.I. Patch me through any way you can to Lieutenant Mculland. He's my bodyguard. . . . . Okay, let me do this . . . . Red card . . . . green card . . . . 007 . . . . click, click, a058323, Patch me through the cellular . . . . okay . . . .

These were his exact words . . .

Officers went out to make sure he was okay . . .

———〰〰〰———

Dispatcher   911, what is your emergency?

Caller   Communists are picking the lock on my door, and placing tiny pebbles in circles and leaving behind onion skins.

———〰〰〰———

Dispatcher   911, what is your emergency?

Caller   A man with no legs or arms is hiding in my chest of drawers

———〰〰〰———

Dispatcher   What is your emergency?

Caller   I was robbed by a picture on a billboard.

Now the guy on the billboard is threatening me.

I can't understand why you can't hear the threats too.

Dispatcher   What did he steal?

Caller   My **dignity** and a can of **chewing tobacco**.

—⧙⧘—

Dispatcher 911, what is your emergency?

Caller   Burglars are hypnotizing me; they move my slippers around and unscrew my cable T.V.

—⧙⧘—

Dispatcher   911, what is your emergency?

Caller   The White House is bugging my phones.

—⧙⧘—

Dispatcher   911, what is your emergency?

Caller   They're injecting me with white itching fluid.

—⧙⧘—

Dispatcher   911, what is your emergency?

Caller   People are jumping in my stomach, trying to rape me.

Dispatcher   911, what is your emergency?

Caller   The upstairs neighbors are using electrical machine equipment with wires trying to shock me.

Dispatcher ... San Diego 911 what is your emergency?

Caller . . .   Take florescent light bulbs, plug it into cable and it will knock out National Security.

Dispatcher   911 what is your emergency?

Caller   There are ghosts coming through the walls.

A 70 year old woman called 911 saying a 'cult' was inside her cookie jar.

The woman's husband got on the line and said his wife had been hallucinating for the past few days, possibly a reaction to her medication.

The husband did not want police or paramedics to come out. He promised to take her to the doctor right away.

———〰———

When the dispatcher first answered this call, she thought it was a valid burglary happening now, with the home owner inside his house.

Dispatcher   911, what is your emergency?

Caller   Some guys are cutting my window screen and coming in the house.

The dispatcher assumed this was a valid burglary 'hot prowl', (occurring now) and connected a three way with her supervisor as the man continued . . .

Caller: Now I hear a gun being loaded, they're gonna shoot me.

The dispatcher's adrenaline is pumping at this point, bracing for a horrific situation. The caller continued

Caller: Now one of them is hiding in the palm tree . . . . Wait a minute, there is a guy sitting on a couch on my porch . . . . how did that couch get on my porch?

At this point, we start to realize the caller might be having some psychiatric issues, or is high on drugs. He mentioned he had a roommate. So we asked if we could talk to his roommate.

Caller: He won't come to the phone, he says it is all my imagination, and I am hallucinating. You see I take medication that makes me hallucinate.

Officers still continued out just to make sure he was okay.

And the dispatcher breathed a sigh of relief . . . .

―――ᗡᗡᒪ―――

A favorite caller of the dispatchers was a sweet woman who would call every few days. She would always say the same thing each time.

Dispatcher   911, what is your emergency?

Caller   My name is (she gave her name) . . . . my address is . . . (she gave her address) . . . . my phone number is . . . . (she gave her phone number) . . . . Electronic vibrating beams are permeating from different parts of my body and are causing damage in my apartment . . . . God Bless you . . . . Good bye

She was a very sweet, lovely woman, and she called for years. When we learned she passed away, we were very saddened. We love you Mrs. M . . . God Bless you . . .

CHAPTER SIX

POOP POOP A DOOP

We answer 911 calls within seconds, but sometimes the non emergency calls have to wait longer if we are busy or short staffed. So many callers will go about their business while waiting for us to answer the line. There are times as I answer the line, I will hear belches, farts and toilets being flushed.

Hey, multi-tasking is a great thing.

Dispatcher   911, what is your emergency?

Caller   It's not going down!

Dispatcher   Are you having a medical problem? (Thinking food might be caught in his throat.)

Caller   No, the **shit** won't go down!

Dispatcher   Are you having a plumbing problem?

Caller   Yes, my toilet is plugged up.

Dispatcher   Well, this is the police department

Caller   I know, do you happen to have a plumber there that's available?

Dispatcher   No, you'll have to call a plumber on your own. Goodbye Sir.

A woman who manages a nursing home, called in to report a man inside one of the bathrooms. He did not live there and she didn't know who he was. During the call, the guy walked out of the bathroom and said he just needed to take a crap. He then walked out the door, and down the street.

Officers went out but were not able to locate him

(I guess when you gotta go . . . You gotta go . . .)

and

(after his poo, he must have had a little more spring in his step, and was able to walk a little faster to elude officers.)

A mother called reporting that her two adult sons were fighting.

One brother **passed gas** when the other brother was eating breakfast.

This offended the 2nd brother who then sprayed the first brother with a household cleaner.

The gassy brother left the house;

The remaining brother got on the phone and said, 'I'm sick of this shit".

A woman called in a noise complaint against her roommate who was **farting**.

During one of our heavy rains, Sorrento Valley Rd. became flooded with about 2 feet of water.

A man called in. He was driving his van through the street and the van lifted up and started floating towards the trees on the side of the road. Two units went out.

When they got out there, they could see one of the drain pipes was clogged causing the flooding.

The canine officer used his dog's "pooper scooper" to unplug the drain.

(Now that's a great use of city equipment.)

Officers responded to an apartment where two female roommates were arguing.

When officers arrived, they found the reason for the argument.

One of the roommates had left a **turd** in the toilet and didn't flush.

One dispatcher joked . . . That's a job for the Tidy Bowl man . . .

Another said . . . That's a plumbing problem . . . They're not supposed to call us when the shits in the toilet, They're supposed to call us when The shit hits the fan . . .

―――∿∿―――

Dispatcher   911 what is your emergency?

Caller   I'm at work.

My roommate just came here, started arguing with me and punched me in the face.

Dispatcher   What was the argument about?

Caller   He said I "**stunk**" up the bathroom, and he wants me to go home and clean it up!

Officers went out to break up the argument.

—⁓—

Dispatcher   San Diego Police, how can I help you?

60 yr old caller My husband missed the toilet and poo-pooed on the floor.

Can you send an officer out to clean it up?

(To protect, serve . . . And clean up after?)

—⁓—

A burglary suspect, who broke into a woman's house, apparently **defecated** in her garage before he left.

Officers came out, took the burglary report and **impounded** the **poop** for possible DNA evidence.

(Cops just don't get paid enough for what they have to do.)

In this case, our caller was number 1; our job was number 2.)

—⁓—

On an episode of the television show COPS, Cleveland Police had a specialized unit that responded to emergency calls.

They were called, "Fast Action Response Team" . . . F.A.R.T. for short . . . .

(Clever, I wonder who came up with that. You gotta love it.)

—ɯ—

Periodically, a representative from the San Diego Gas and Electric Company will call in to advise us of a procedure they routinely conduct. We will then type up the information for all dispatchers and officers in the area in case concerned citizens call us. We will then format an F.Y.I. something like this:

"SDGE will be blowing natural gas into the atmosphere for about 30 minutes in case anyone calls in to report smelling gas."

CHAPTER SEVEN

FASHIONISTAS

A caller called 911 to report a man out on the street, exposing himself to passersby . . .

The witness gave the following description of the suspect.

White male, 40, 5'7. heavy set, wearing a **pink tutu and tight shorts**.

(Try to picture it . . .

. . . Now you'll never get that picture out of your mind.)

Officers responded to a mother-daughter disturbance call.

The mother called saying her 17 year old daughter was refusing to go to school.

The daughter then got on the phone, yelling at her mother and crying.

The daughter told the dispatcher she did not want to go to school because she wanted to get highlights in her hair and the beauty shop was still closed.

———~m~———

A woman called to report a male transvestite prostitute flagging down people driving by in cars.

Officers responded. When they arrived on scene, the officers gave the dispatcher the following description of the guy's ensemble . . .

Attractive sunflower dress and matching shirt along with contrasting red, blue and yellow sandals.

Officers contacted him, he agreed to leave and not return.

———~m~———

Often witnesses working in the clothing retail business have a unique eye for fashion. It is apparent when they are giving suspect information.

Here are a couple examples of our GQ callers . . . .

A store employee called from a clothing store to report a shoplifter.

When the dispatcher asked for the suspect's description, the fashion savvy saleswoman said,

"She looks Hispanic . . . 24 yrs old . . . . **size 12.**"

—m—

Here is another one . . .

A clothing store employee called in to report a male walking around the complex that looked suspicious and thought the guy might be planning on robbing the business.

The witness described the suspect as a white male, 20's, 5'9, thin, **32 inch waist, mauve shirt, teal green pants.**

(This guy knows his business . . . he should be employee of the month.)

—m—

We received a call from a security officer reporting a naked male.

The guy was covered with oil, and wrapped in Saran Wrap. He was "flashing" people as they arrived to work.

Officers went out, and took a field interview. He promised to leave and not do this again; so they let him go on his way.

(A field interview is a short report with the subject's basic information and the circumstances. It's not a permanent report. It is written up in case there are any problems with him in the near future.)

—⟶ɯ⟵—

(Just a word of advice . . .
Don't be a fashion critic with friends . . .)

Jim Jones and John Smith were inside the convenience store, teasing each other about the clothing they were wearing.

The teasing turned into arguing. The arguing escalated into fighting, and the guys took it outside.

John Smith stabbed Jones multiple times.

Jones was transported by paramedics to the hospital, and Smith was taken to County Jail.

—⟶ɯ⟵—

Dispatcher   911, what is your emergency?

Caller   A guy is sitting in a silver compact. When anyone walks by, he jumps out of the car and exposes himself.

Dispatcher   What is he wearing?

Caller   **A black jacket, peach teddy top, black garter, and no underwear.**

CHAPTER EIGHT

SOME LIKE US, SOME DON'T

Each dispatcher takes hundreds of calls each day during their shift. Most citizens are cooperative and appreciate our help.

Often, there are those who are irate, uncooperative and yell obscenities throughout the call. We try to stay professional regardless of the badgering, and just let the caller vent.

But we are human, and once in a while a dispatcher will have enough.

Here is an example:

A dispatcher was patiently listening to a male caller. He was ranting and raving, cussing at her throughout a non emergency call. He used the 'F' word every chance he got.

She warned him several times to stop cussing at her, but he ignored her request. Finally she said . . . .

"That's it! **3 Fuck You's is** my limit!!!!! I'm disconnecting."

And with that the dispatcher hung up.

—⁓〰⁓—

Communications is staffed 7 days a week, 24 hours a day. If a holiday falls on a dispatchers regular work day, they need to work the holiday.

It's nice when a citizen thanks us or shows they appreciate us for being there.

Here is an example . . .

The World Series was being played one day.

Everyone was celebrating.

A guy called in to thank us for all we do and to say he is sorry we have to work when everyone else gets to party.

That was very much appreciated. The dispatcher that took the call sent the message around the room and saved it for the next shift to read.

When I grew up, I was taught to respect your elders and authority.

Today, most young people still show respect and compassion for others.

However, now-a-days, some young teens show an attitude and disrespect for teachers, elders and Law Enforcement.

Here is an example . . .

This 13 yr old girl was screaming profanities throughout the call.

Dispatcher: San Diego 911, what is your emergency?

13 yr old girl:**GET A F . . . ING COP OUT HERE NOW!!**

Dispatcher: What is your address?

Teen: You can see the address,

JUST GET THE F . . . K OUT HERE!

Dispatcher: Police are coming, but I need more information, what is going on there?

Teen: **I'm not telling you nothing' else, just get the f . . . k out here NOW!**

And she hung up.

Officers were dispatched for an unknown emergency.

This puts officers and citizens at risk. The responding officers cannot be prepared to take the precautions needed for everyone's safety.

Fortunately, this call was only two guys fist fighting outside. No weapons involved.

Some citizens are not happy with our response time on busy nights . . .

A guy called to report a fist fight. A couple minutes later he called back because the officers had not showed up yet. He was very upset and said,

"What's it gonna take to get a cop out here?! I can get a pizza delivered faster than this!"

Many of you might remember the infamous tank chase in May of 1995. The footage was aired on television stations across the United States.

On May 18th, 1995, a U.S. Army veteran simply drove into the United States National Guard Armory located in San Diego, and stole a 53 ton M60a3 Patton tank. There was a push button on the tank to start the ignition. And just like that, he drove off in the tank and began a terrifying rampage that could have killed hundreds of people.

He barreled down a residential street. He destroyed parked cars, motorhomes and charged towards a house. He hit occupied vehicles and ran over a fire hydrant shooting water high into the air.

At one point he deliberately tried taking down a pedestrian bridge by ramming the support beams several times. He finally gave up on knocking down the bridge and headed towards the freeway. The officers knew once he got on the freeway he could mow down hundreds of occupied vehicles.

He entered State Route 163 and continued his rampage down the freeway.

San Diego Police and California Highway Patrol officers were in hot pursuit but had no idea how they were going to stop that tank. Officers also did not know if the guns on the tank were loaded.

Everyone and everything in his path were at this man's mercy.

About a half a mile down freeway, he suddenly turned the tank to cross over into oncoming traffic.

Fortunately, the tank got stuck on the freeway median.

The officers realized this was probably going to be their only chance to stop this guy.

Risking their own lives, the brave officers rushed the tank. One of the officers was able to open the hatch not knowing if the suspect was armed.

The suspect refused to comply and one of the brave officers was forced to shoot him.

The suspect later died at the hospital.

He had the potential of killing hundreds of people that day, using a 57 ton tank as his deadly weapon.

Now, you would think that all citizens would have been grateful to the officers who risked their lives to stop this man from killing innocent people.

Most people were grateful. But surprisingly, there were citizens who actually called into 911 Communications to complain and criticize the officer who shot the suspect. I took a couple of those complaint calls myself.

I wonder what those same people would have said if officers did not stop the suspect before he killed scores of innocent victims. Or if these complainants would have risked their lives to save people as these officers did.

Cops often are "damned if they do and damned if they don't." No matter what they do, someone will criticize their actions.

Please note: These views are my own and not necessarily those of the San Diego Police Department.

CHAPTER NINE

AGE IS JUST A NUMBER

A woman called 911 to say she was going to jump off a bridge because she just turned 30. We responded to get her help.

(Hopefully, after counseling she realized there is life after 30.)

———〰———

Dispatcher   911, what is your emergency?

Witness   There are two elderly women fighting over a purse at a bus stop.

Officers went out and broke up the fight.

(Wow, the two feisty broads can still pack a punch.)

———〰———

A white female, 65 years old, 5'5", 140lbs, gray hair, wearing a multicolor long sleeve top, and beige pants had been in a psychiatric facility.

She was schizophrenic and severely mentally impaired.

But she sure was in good shape!

She escaped the facility by jumping a fence and high-tailing it out of there.

A concerned friend called 911 to say she hadn't heard from her friend all afternoon.

She was worried the woman might have fallen. Her friend is 104 years old.

When officers got out to the friends house, they found her going for a leisurely walk in the courtyard.

(Wow, good for her!)

We got a call from a senior center of two elderly women fighting. A 92 year old hit an 83 year old with a load of bread.

(Why doesn't she pick on someone her own age?)

A spunky woman in her 80's called, very upset at what she had to witness everyday when she would catch her bus.

The same young man was always there, with his pants hanging so low that his buttocks showed.

She told the dispatcher, "I feel like getting a sling shot and shooting his back end. Who wants to see that?!"

She went on to say,

"Today I told him . . . . For heaven's sake, pull up your pants!!!!"

CHAPTER TEN

THE THONG GUY

We all love the beach, and officers work hard at keeping it family-friendly.

However there is an infamous, free spirit, dubbed "The Thong Guy".

He is often seen roller-blading up and down the boardwalk wearing only a thong. Sometimes, he wears less. Most local beach goers are familiar with him.

His 'clothing is optional' attitude, however, often shocks tourists.

He always seems to elude police.

Here are some examples,

Take a minute to stop and picture it. You will have to laugh . . . .

One Thanksgiving Day, a shocked tourist called to report a naked man rollerblading northbound on the boardwalk.

She described him as:

"A white male, 40's, 6'2", 180 lbs., wearing only a **top hat, his rear painted green and a picture of a turkey painted on his penis.**"

—⁓∿⁓—

Same guy, different day . . . .

We got a call of a white male rollerblading down the boardwalk, wearing a **"wig, silver shorts, and a silver halter top."**

—⁓∿⁓—

Same guy, different day, 4th of July . . .

A tourist called in on same guy,

White male rollerblading down the boardwalk, wearing **red, white and blue, with a beer can covering his penis.**

—⁓∿⁓—

Same guy, different day . . . .

A witness called to report the same guy,

On rollerblades, nude, with a **white bulls-eye painted on his buttocks, a beer can on his testicles, and a half moon on his head.**

Once again, he was able to elude police.

CHAPTER ELEVEN

MAN'S BEST FRIENDS

A pet owner called, requesting an officer come out and **smell** her dog.

She went on to explain that her dog had been scratching constantly and she was afraid he got sprayed by a skunk.

The caller said she has no sense of smell.

She needs the officer to come out and smell the dog so he doesn't stink up the house.

―――〰―――

A woman called because her veterinarian's office only has two parking spaces, and no spaces reserved for patients.

She had to park across the street and walk her pig back to the Dr.'s office.

The caller wanted to know if she could get a handicapped placard for her **pig.**

―――〰―――

Dispatcher   San Diego 911, what is your emergency?

<u>Caller</u>   My nephew gave my son's pet iguana beer and now the iguana is not moving.

She was advised to take the iguana to a veterinarian.

———ɯ———

We got a call from a citizen reporting a hazard. A cow was walking down the middle of the road. This is in a rural area, and the cow must have escaped from an opening in the fence.

(When officers got out there, they probably asked the cow to 'moo've over.)

———ɯ———

San Diego Police Code Enforcement Unit usually handles Municipal Code violations in neighborhoods.

A Code Compliance Officer was approached by a dog looking for help.

The dog, who we learned later was called Ziggy, got the officers attention and then took off.

Ziggy ran so fast, the officer had to run to catch up with him three times.

The dog finally stopped running, and the officer saw another dog, who was stuck in a fence hole, 4 feet above the ground and was hanging by its back legs.

The officer climbed the fence. He got the dog down, plugged up the hole in the fence and secured both dogs in the backyard.

The rescued dog had a dog tag with the name, "Cashmere".

The officer later joked to the dispatcher . . . . Tell the dog owner he owes me dry cleaning for the all the mud and mess the dogs did to me.

(Kudos to Ziggy . . . Lassie would be proud.)

———

A reluctant woman called to complain about very loud music coming from a neighbor's house.

She said she hates to call about something like this, but the noise is so loud, that both she and her cat are throwing up, and she just can't take it anymore.

———

We got a 911 call from a woman screaming at the top of her lungs, she wasn't saying anything, just screaming.

Finally, after several minutes, she let us know that she was on top of her kitchen table, and there was a mouse running around her kitchen.

We referred her to an exterminator and cancelled the call.

The owner of a Great Dane called because his neighbor was chasing his dog with a spiked metal object.

The neighbor said the Great Dane had just killed her cat.

The officers responded, got out of the car and began talking to both neighbors.

One of the officers looked back and saw that the Great Dane had jumped into the police car.

When the officer walked back to the car, the Great Dane, sitting up in the driver's seat, turned his head toward the officer and flashed a "big smile" on it's face.

(I guess when you're a Great Dane; you can sit whereever you want.)

Dispatcher   911, what is your emergency?

Frantic female I think someone is on my roof, and it
                    sounds like they are trying to break my
                    window.

Officers rushed over. After arriving on the scene, they concluded no one was trying to break into her house. The officer humorously commented to the radio dispatcher,

I have a visual of 20-30 blackbirds that were on her roof. They are now in the wind (flying away). No need to notify Gang Unit (since the gang of birds were no longer congregating.)

(A cat burglar . . . ?)

We got a call from a person who was hearing noises outside his house. He thought someone was trying to break into his house.

It turns out, the so-called burglar was a cat that had a tin can stuck on its head and he couldn't get it off.

The radio dispatcher asked the officer . . . .

<u>Dispatcher</u> . . . "Well, did you get the can off his head?"

<u>Officer</u>   "Affirm, but he just took off without saying thank you, the ungrateful ingrate . . . ."

It was a slow night for officers when an alarm company called.

The alarm company was monitoring audio from one of their customers. This means they are able to hear what is going on inside and outside the business.

Officers got out to the business, and determined the noise was coming from a guard dog.

The guard dog was in the yard, dragging around a large plastic trash lid.

The officer commented . . .

"I guess the dog was bored too."

———ᗰ———

An officer called into our Communications center for assistance. He reported the following:

"I'm on a dog-napping caper.

The suspects stole a 5 month old pit bull from a parking lot . . . .

The suspects had just filled out job applications at a nearby store . . . could we have officers go by the home addresses they gave to attempt to locate the suspects and dog?"

(It's probably a sure bet those guys won't be getting one of those job positions . . . don't ya think?)

A young wife called at 4:00 in the morning.

She was concerned that her 24 year old husband had left the house at 11:00 the night before to walk their Springer spaniel and had not returned.

She called the jails, friends, and hospitals, and still could not locate him.

Police searched the area, and found her husband. He was still walking the dog in the rain. He was fine. Officers told him to go home to let his wife know he was okay.

(Wow, a six hour walk!)

Officers went out on an alarm call at a business.

Officers cautiously walked up to the closed business.

Suddenly five Dobermans came out of the gated storage area. The gate was open.

Luckily, the dogs were friendly.

The officer joked . . .

"I was trying to say C-4 (everything was okay), while the 5 dogs were jumping on me, waging their tails."

A witness called in, said a man was hitting a woman with what appeared to be a sword.

The woman was lying in the street.

The witness then said the victim was walking away and the suspect got into a van.

Officers quickly got on scene and stopped the van.

When they looked inside, they saw a cobra snake.

Another officer hearing the call over the radio, advised cobras will spit and to use caution.

Officers found the victim, who had minor scratches.

Officers evaluated the call for about an hour.

It was not a domestic violence, or assault with a weapon crime.

She claimed the man was using the snake for some type of voodoo, and said she was a willing participant.

The woman refused medical help or to make a citizen's arrest.

So no report was taken, and both parties went on their way . . .

—ɯ—

A commercial burglar alarm went off at a well known eating establishment.

After officers responded they cancelled the incident with the following explanation;

"No burglary, just **rodents** that set off the motion sensors."

—ɯ—

We do our best to help get help to animals that are injured. Sometimes, however, getting the correct people to respond is not always that easy. Here is an example,

9:08 a.m.   We received a call from another police agency to assist in a car accident that occurred in their city.

The driver hit a llama, severely injuring it.

The driver was being evaluated for driving under the influence of alcohol.

She claimed she had been raped, and was trying to escape the suspect when she hit the llama.

9:09 a.m.   One of our sergeants and a traffic unit were advised and started responding to the other city to assist.

9:10 a.m.   Our dispatchers began contacting an animal agency to help the llama.

9:23 a.m.   The other police agency advised us the llama was dead.

9:27 a.m.   San Diego Animal Regulations Unit advised us they would not respond because the llama was dead.

9:28 a.m.   Our Shops Division was advised to respond to pick up the dead llama and dispose of it.

9:31 a.m.   The officer on scene now says the llama might still be alive, and requested a veterinarian.

9:40 a.m.   We again contacted the Animal Regulations Unit to let them know the llama might still be alive. They told us they only respond to domestic animals and referred us to an animal agency called, "Fund for Animals".

9:40 a.m.   We contacted Fund for Animals who told us they are only allowed to respond to wild animals. Since the the llama is someone's pet, it is viewed as a domestic animal (such a horse).

9:41 a.m.   We then contacted the Humane Society to see if they could help. The said they would send someone out. It would take them about 30 minutes to get there. The Human Society asked us to let them know if the owner of the llama shows up, or if the llama dies.

9:42 a.m. Our lead dispatcher is still checking for a veterinarian to respond on the injured llama.

9:43 a.m. The zoo was notified and said they knew a veterinarian that might be able to respond.

9:44 a.m. The officer from the other agency advised the llama did die.

All agencies and units involved were then notified.

A person called because she heard two women screaming as if they were in pain.

Officers went out to the location to try and find the women. The officers did find them.

It turns out the ladies had been screaming because they saw a spider!

A woman called 911 because she was hearing noises and thumps on the side of her house.

She thought someone might be breaking into her house.

When officers got out there, they found cats all over the place.

It turns out the caller makes ceramic figures out of dead fish molds.

The officers said it smelled like a seafood restaurant in the yard. They tried to shoo the cats away, but the cats weren't budging.

Dispatcher   911 what is your emergency?

Caller   I hear a woman screaming and slapping sounds. I think someone is getting beat up.

It turns out a possum jumped on a neighbor's head as she went to get something in her kitchen.

She was screaming and slapping herself to get the thing off of her head.

An alarm company called in to report an alarm going off at a residence.

Dispatchers always ask if there are any pets that live inside the house.

The alarm company advised there was a cat that lived there.

The dispatcher joked,

"In case any canine units are responding . . . no eating on the job."

A woman called in to report a mother duck and several ducklings were stranded on a center divide of a busy street.

Officers found the ducks and stopped traffic.

Drivers and on-lookers watched and smiled as officers gently guided them to safety.

The manager of an apartment complex called because a rottweiler kept coming onto the complex.

The dog would walk around, and growl at the tenants.

It turns out this rottweiler was a new mom, and one of the tenants in this building had bought one of her puppies.

(Sounds like the new mom just wanted to see her little pup.)

—⁓—

A suspect, running from police ran down a canyon with the police in hot pursuit.

But the officers were not the only ones that stopped him. The suspect was bitten by a rattlesnake.

He was taken into custody and treated for the snakebite.

(It's nice to see our reptile friends getting involved).

—⁓—

Dispatcher: San Diego Police. #160, what are you reporting?

Caller   My pet bird was stolen from the beach. He is worth $13,000.

(Gees, I hope his bird lays golden eggs!)

—⁓—

A conscientious woman wanted to notify us of a party she was planning at the beach.

She had gotten a noise permit, and was going to be having a live band.

The permit was from 1200-1900 hours (noon-7 p.m.)

It was a birthday party for her English Bull Dog who just turned one year old.

(Lucky dog!)

CHAPTER TWELVE

SERIOUSLY?!

An employee of a fast food restaurant called for police.

An irate woman was in the drive-thru refusing to leave.

The woman was upset over the amount of ice cream they put in her cone.

—⁓⁓—

A man called 911 because he wanted police to get more alcohol for him.

—⁓⁓—

Another male called 911 requesting a pizza.

—⁓⁓—

A woman called 911 to ask if the San Diego Chargers were playing tomorrow.

—⁓⁓—

A woman called to ask if her dog would count as a person for the car pool.

A woman called for a burglary report. She said someone broke into her house and stole her marijuana.

Officers went out, but did not take a burglary report.

(Gutsy . . .)

A woman called police because some kids in front of her house were making "Woody WoodPecker" impersonations . . . .

(What the heck does that mean?)

It's probably not a good idea to give vanity a priority over a medical emergency . . .

Dispatcher   911, what is your emergency?

Caller   I think I'm having a heart attack

Dispatcher   How old are you?

Caller   I'd rather not say, there is someone else in the room with me.

A woman called very upset, to complain that the police helicopter had been flying around her house for the past two weeks.

She claimed the noise has been so loud that it harasses her dogs.

She went on to say, it is such a problem that she and her husband are now sleeping in separate bedrooms and are headed for divorce.

Dispatcher   911, what is your emergency?

Caller   I am a tourist from Germany. I hope you can help me. I had sex last night and forgot my 'morning after' pills at home. I am afraid I will become pregnant.

A woman called for officers to come out.

She said she put a bagel in a 4 slot toaster.

When she returned 10 minutes later, the bagel was in a different slot.

The caller was sure someone came in and moved it.

A man called because he gave a guy $40 to buy some marijuana for him and the guy never came back.

The caller said he was hesitant to call, but he had to make a theft report or his boyfriend would be very angry at him for losing the money.

An officer went out, but did not take a report.

A man saw an officer on the street and stopped him.

He asked if the officer would give him directions to his house so he could then give the directions to his son who was coming to visit.

The officer asked him, "why not drive the route yourself and write down the street names yourself?"

The man admitted that would mean he'd have to get in his car and drive there and back. He didn't want to take the time.

An irate customer called 911 from a taco shop because there wasn't enough cheese in his nachos.

An unhappy customer from a fast food restaurant called 911 because she didn't get any chicken in her chicken salad.

———〰———

An irate customer called 911 from a fast food restaurant because she got cold french fries and the employees won't refund her money

———〰———

An angry man called 911 claiming the police officer stole his dentures.

———〰———

Dispatcher   911 What is your emergency?

Caller   I need money

Dispatcher   Sorry, sir, we don't have extra money to give away

Caller   Then can you give me the phone number to the Mafia?

Dispatcher   You will have to call 411 for directory assistance.

Caller   Thank you.

And with that he hung up.

A man called 911 to report the air conditioning inside a fast food restaurant was up so high, a person could catch pneumonia.

The dispatcher told him to speak with the store manager.

We received a call from a woman who was very upset.

She wanted the police to "preserve the peace" at a place where she just bought some dope.

She said the dope she bought wasn't quality stuff for what she paid for it. So she wanted the police to help her get her money back.

The officers did go out, but not for what she requested.

An angry neighbor called to complain about the couple in the apartment next to her. She said they are always too loud when they have sex.

She asked if officers could contact them and asked them to keep it down.

When officers eventually got out there, all was quiet. Therefore, they did not contact the couple and went on to the next call.

———∭———

A woman asked if officers could 'preserve the peace' and go with her to a jeweler while he works on her rings because she doesn't trust him.

CHAPTER THIRTEEN

BLOOPERS

We often abbreviate words when typing out a call (formatting). We use specific abbreviations that are used by all dispatchers for uniformity and clarity.

But a dispatcher trainee learned what not to abbreviate in the following call:

A bail bondsman went to a house and knocked on the door. He displayed an I.D. when the resident answered the door.

He said he was about to apprehend a fugitive and asked her to call the police for assistance.

The resident complied and called 911 saying, a bail bondsman was at her door asking for **assistance.**

The dispatcher trainee typed:

"Bail bondsman just came to resident's door asking for **ass.**"

(You gotta be careful when using abbreviations . . .)

Dispatchers type throughout the day, and need to be accurate.

From time to time, we will make typos. Here are some examples . . .

A typo from a dispatcher at California Highway Patrol . . .

"Interstate 5 at Interstate 805 a white male is **under** a **bride** . . ."

(I think he meant bridge.)

We got an alarm call from Saks Department Store, in an upscale shopping center. The male dispatcher spelled the name of the business, "Sachs".

(You can tell a male dispatcher typed up that call, and his wife probably does his shopping for him.)

When anyone calls from a cell phone, the caller's location is not displayed on our computer screen. So we have to get their exact location from the caller. This dispatcher had an embarrassing blooper moment . . . .

A man was calling in a crime.

Dispatcher: San Diego 911, what are you reporting?

Caller: I'm at **Brighton** and **Bacon**

Dispatcher: Sir, I know you are frightened and naked, but I need to know where you are.

Caller: No! I'm not **frightened** and **naked**, I'm at **Brighton** (Ave.**)** and **Bacon** (St.**)**!!!!

CHAPTER FOURTEEN

LOST IN TRANSLATION

A witness was calling in a crime. The dispatcher started asking the initial questions to get a physical description of the suspect.

Dispatcher Was he White, Black or Hispanic?

Witness (after a long pause) . . . I think he was **Presbyterian**.

―――⁂―――

Dispatcher: San Diego Police, #160, what are you reporting?

Australian Visitor: I'd like to report a loud potty.

The dispatcher figured out he was reporting a loud **party**.

―――⁂―――

Dispatcher San Diego Police, how can I help you?

Caller: A car is blocking my driveway, and I need to leave.

The police were out here last night and arrested the driver.

I think he was arrested for an **IUD** (Intra-Uterine Device).

(I think she meant DUI (Driving Under the Influence).

———ɯɯ———

Dispatcher   911, what is your emergency?

Caller   I want to report kids that might be getting ready to tag something, (graffiti).

I see 5 juveniles running down the street **"shaking their cans"** . . .

———ɯɯ———

A Good Samaritan saw a man lying unconscious on the ground and called the police for help . . .

Dispatcher   911, what is your emergency?

Woman caller There is a man laying on the ground, I am trying to **arouse** him.

———ɯɯ———

Sometimes when a caller has a heavy accent, it takes a little clarifying to get the correct information . . .

<u>Dispatcher</u>	What is your emergency?
<u>Accent Caller</u>	There's a guy at 14th and "K" shooting in front of the building.
<u>Dispatcher</u>	Is he shooting a gun?
<u>Accent Caller</u>	NO! Not **shooting**, **shitting** . . . . He's got his pants down and the son-of-a-bitch is shitting right in front of the building!!

When dispatchers answer 911 calls, we are supposed to identify ourselves with either our first name or dispatcher number.

That became a problem with Dispatcher #108.

When she would answer, "911 #108, some callers would scream back . . . "NO, I won't wait!"

She had to change from using her dispatch number to using her name.

Nurses fill a very important role in the medical field. A large percentage of nurses in San Diego are of Filipino decent. They consistently provide patients with exceptional, compassionate care.

Usually, the language barrier is not a factor. Once in awhile, however, it might not be the case . . . .

———⚍———

My son, Mike was an E.M.T. (Emergency Medical Technician) for several years. Here are a couple of calls he got when he first started. This is how it played out in his words.

We responded to a call from a Nursing Home.

They called because there was an emergency with one of their patients.

I was new at the time; it was one of my first calls. I wanted to get as much information as I could so when we got to the hospital we could give it to the doctor.

I asked the nurse what medications the patient was on.

In a heavy Filipino accent, she said, '**Oh, he taka da peena butta ball.**"

I was little perplexed, and repeated what I heard,

"Peanut Butter Ball?"

Now if I had been seasoned, I would have known to second guess it. But I just assumed it was some type of a vitamin supplement, or protein supplement.

So I asked her again . . . . "Peanut Butter Ball?"

She said "Yes, da peena butta ball".

So I wrote on my paperwork that gets attached to the call, and gets turned into County E.M.S. (Emergency Medical Service), with my signature on it, forever and all times . . . . **Peanut Butter Ball** written under list of medications.

When we get to the hospital, my patient is out, not really conscious where he could help.

So I'm ready to turn over the patient to the doctor. Everything is going great.

I'm getting the patient's vital signs, and I'm giving all the information I have on the patient to the doctor.

When I got to his list of medications, I said,

"The patient just takes Peanut Butter Balls."

As I'm giving the information, the doctors and nurses are taking off his shirt . . . getting him on an EKG . . . they are about to start an I.V . . . they're trying to read his heart rhythms . . . trying to figure out what is going on . . . . they're looking up his history . . . . there was a lot going on . . . .

But when I said, "Peanut Butter Ball" it was like time stood still . . . .

Because the moment I said, "Peanut Butter Ball", everybody stopped and looked at me like, what the hell is a peanut butter ball!!

Then I knew something was terribly wrong. I turned to look at my partner, and he was laughing so hard in the corner.

It turned out the patient had a history of seizures and takes Phenobarbital.

———ᘓ———

Another call Mike went on . . . .

Probably the same nurse, same heavy Filipino accent . . .

I was still new . . . . we got a call to go to the same nursing home to pick up a patient.

It was a 'code 3' response, with lights and sirens.

When we got there, we stopped, got out, and ran over to the nurse's station to find out who our patient was and what was wrong.

The nurse said, "oh, chicken breath".

And I asked, "Chicken breath?, What is chicken breath?" Is he choking?"

She said, "No, chicken breath."

So we run to the guy's room, and he was totally short of breath,

And the nurse said, "See chicken breath" . . .

Which translated to . . . . "He can't breathe!"

———ɯɯ———

A young boy called 911 to say his **dog** was choking.

The dispatcher thought he said his **dad** was choking. So she told him to put his arms around the stomach (for Heimlich Maneuver).

The boy seemed a little confused and asked, "You mean **between** his **legs**?"

The dispatcher exclaimed, "**NO!**"

The dispatcher soon realized the boy was talking about his dog,

Don't worry, the dog made it . . .

———ɯɯ———

A very elderly female called 911 asking for paramedics.

The dispatcher asked her what her address was to confirm the location that was displayed on the computer screen.

She said she had just moved in a month ago and could not remember what her address was.

The dispatcher then asked if there was any **mail** around her house that would indicate the new address.

The woman quickly responded . . . "No, I don't have a **male** here!"

—⚏—

Dispatcher   What is your emergency?

Frantic caller   Baby's in the dryer!!

Dispatcher   Your **baby** is in the dryer?

Caller   Yes, baby's in the dryer! She must have crawled in.

The dryer might have been going for about 20 minutes.

She was hysterical. After asking more questions, the dispatcher realized "Baby" is the name of her pet dog.

(The dog was okay, but maybe they should change his name to Fluffy.)

—⚏—

We often ask callers to spell words phonetically to be sure we get it right. We use standard words that are used by all dispatchers and police.

But the public will usually use the first words that come to their mind. Here are three examples.

One caller gave the following . . . .

"W" like **Wyoming** . . . . "U" like **ugly** . . . . ☺

Another caller was giving a license plate phonetically . . . he didn't think simple . . . .

"Z" as in **zip code** . . . . "N" as in **nuts** . . . .
"S" as in **Sukiyaki**

Another caller gave . . . .

"P" as in **party** . . . . "D" as in **Dora**

(She must have kids . . .)

———〰〰〰———

A guy called in to report an on-going problem.

Every night when I walk home I am confronted by the same homeless man. The guy always seems to be drunk. He follows me down the street and yells things about my **mother**.

(Perhaps he is saying . . . mother f . . . r???)

CHAPTER FIFTEEN

DUMB AND DUMBER

A neighbor called in to report a young woman fell backwards out of a 2nd story window.

The caller said the fall appeared to be accidental.

When officers got there the young woman was conscious and transported to the hospital. She suffered head and neck abrasions but was going to be okay.

It turns out she had been by the window, "**mooning**" people on the street when she fell out of the window.

A carjacker came up to his victim and ordered him out of the car, then drove off in the stolen vehicle.

Unfortunately for the suspect, he did not know how to drive a **stick shift**.

The victim had the gear in reverse, so the suspect drove the car in reverse at least three blocks until he was out of sight.

(He was going westbound at the time, and was near the beach. So, if he continued into the ocean, he will turn up at high tide.)

We got a call from a hysterical woman who called from a fast food restaurant restroom.

She said her estranged husband had kidnapped her.

Before police officers arrived, the suspect had left the restaurant.

Police found him a short while later getting a pedicure at a nearby salon and arrested him.

(At least his feet will look good in prison.)

We received a call from the San Diego County Sheriff's Office.

They requested extra patrol by several of our units around the Coroner's Office that night.

The Sheriff's Department has jurisdiction over the Coroner's Office.

An employee from the Coroner's Office reported a male had made phone threats. The suspect said he would come over there that day and not be responsible for what happens.

The suspect is known to them, and has made similar threats in the past.

(Police put extra patrol around the Coroner's Office as a precaution. But didn't this guy realize most of the people there were already dead?!!)

———〰〰———

A man drove through the drive-thru at a fast food restaurant.

When the employee asked for his order, he said, "I'm gonna rob you".

He then continued through the drive-thru, parked his car, went inside the restaurant and ordered his food.

He didn't mention anything else about the robbery.

(I guess he has a very short attention span.)

———〰〰———

(This guy is either very brave or very stupid . . .)

A witness called from a payphone reporting **one** guy challenging approximately **15 bikers** to a fight!!

———〰〰———

A sales lady from a department store called 911.

A guy went into the housewares department and stole napkin rings.

Then, he put the napkin rings around his penis and exposed himself to the sales lady.

The suspect was gone by the time officers got out there, so they just took a report.

(I doubt the store would have wanted those napkin rings back anyway.)

—⁓—

A few days before Thanksgiving, a mother called to say her 35 year old son stole the frozen turkey she was going to prepare for Thanksgiving dinner.

She explained her son is on drugs, and she thought he might try to pawn the turkey for drug money.

(Gees, look what drugs will have a son stoop so low to do,)

—⁓—

Dispatcher   911, what is your emergency?

Caller   A man jumped my fence. I saw him bang on my window, and make obscene gestures. Then, he took off northbound down the street.

As officers approached him, he '**mooned**' the officers. Not a smart thing to do.

The mooner was soon arrested.

A man was being arrested for driving a stolen vehicle. As the vehicle was being impounded, the suspect asked if he could get his things out of the car.

(Aahhh . . . NO!)

A man called and explained that his television had been stolen from his house a week earlier.

Today, a woman came up to him as he walked by and asked if he wanted to buy a T.V.

He recognized it as the same T.V. that had been stolen from his house.

The officers went out and contacted the clueless burglary suspect.

The manager of a business called in. He wanted to report a guy that came in to apply for a job.

While in the store, the prospective employee accidentally dropped several blank checks belonging to different people.

Officers responded.

(Not a good way to impress a prospective employer.)

An employee of a sandwich shop called in.

A man went into the sandwich shop . . . . he ordered a beef melt, grabbed the sandwich and took off without paying for it.

The problem for the suspect?

He forgot he was wearing a work name badge.

It didn't take long for officers to find the guy and arrest him.

A nurse in a doctor's office called to report that a locked bag with medical specimens and tissue biopsies had been stolen from their office.

The bag had a lock and chain on it.

(The suspects probably thought they were getting a real bag of loot. (surprise, surprise)

A man walked into the bank to rob it.

He used his deposit slip as a demand note.

He did tear off his name and address before giving it to the teller.

However, his account number was still on the deposit slip.

Officers had little problem finding the suspect and arresting him.

A guy got out of jail in San Diego.

He lives in Temecula and needed a ride home.

So he stole a car to get up there.

He got stopped . . . arrested again, and ended up going back to jail in San Diego.

(Hasn't he heard of public transportation?)

A clerk from an adult shop call to say he was just robbed.

What did the suspect take?

A penis enlarger, valued at $160.

(If he stole it because he was embarrassed taking it to the counter to pay for it, imagine how embarrassed he is going to be going to court about it.

Or having to explain every time he is asked, "Have you ever been arrested? If so, explain for what?)

—◊—

(Dumb crook or savvy crook?)

A burglar broke into a house.

He ransacked it, loaded his pockets and stacked the goods by the front door.

At some point, he did his drugs, and passed out in the house.

Police responded . . . .

The suspect's defense to the cops . . . .since he did not get outside of the house with the items, it was not considered burglary, and they could not arrest him on a burglary charge.

A female transient called 911.

She had been sleeping in a dumpster. The garbage truck driver was not aware the woman was in it. She didn't wake up until the truck driver dumped her out at the city dump with all the garbage.

The officers went out and contacted the woman at the city dump.

She was not injured. They offered to take her back to Pacific Beach where she originated.

But as they were standing with her, a pack of amphetamines fell out of a cigarette she had.

So, instead of a free ride back to P.B., she got a one-way ride to jail.

Officers and paramedics responded to a house for a medical call.

When they arrived, they determined the woman was not having a medical emergency.

But she was having a garage sale.

Police were familiar with her. She had mental problems, and officers had contacted her on numerous occasions.

Soon it was determined that she had recently broken into a neighbor house and was now selling all of her neighbor's belongings at that garage sale.

CHAPTER SIXTEEN

SHOULDN'T I BE GETTING HAZARDOUS PAY FOR THIS JOB?

A home owner called to report a prowler.

He saw a man with a ladder climb onto his roof.

The caller said he kicked the ladder to the ground to trap the would-be burglar on his roof until police got out there.

In the meantime, we got another call from a neighbor, reporting that a **cable guy** was stuck on a customer's roof. She said the cable guy was waving his arms in the air and asking for someone to call police . . . .

(Oops . . . a case of mistaken identity . . . and maybe the cable company should have a shorter response time window so the customer doesn't forget they are coming out.)

A barber called in.

One of his customers did not like the haircut he just got and made threats to return and hurt the barber.

Officers in the area were advised of the information and the barber was advised to call back on 911 if this guy returned.

An apartment manager called when he discovered a **severed pig's head** on his balcony.

A robbery suspect walked into a beauty supply shop and attempted to rob them.

One of the victims body slammed the suspect and hit him over the head with a curling iron.

The suspect was arrested.

(Don't underestimate the strength or guts of a great hairdresser!)

A man walked into a posh La Jolla art gallery with a gun. He demanded the woman put all the money from the safe into a bag.

The woman defiantly said, "No, I will not!! Get out of here".

The surprised would-be bandit turned around and walked out.

(We don't recommend you do this of course.)

CHAPTER SEVENTEEN

OOPS

A husband and wife went to a restaurant and parked the car they had just bought in the parking lot. It was a used 1977 model.

When they left the restaurant, the wife found what she thought was their car in the lot. The key opened the door, and started the ignition. When she got home, she realized the car looked identical to her car.

In the meantime, the actual owners reported the car stolen.

Officers went out and cleared up the confusion.

We received a call from an alarm company for an alarm that was going off at a fitness center.

When the operator from the alarm company called inside the business, a frantic woman answered.

The woman said she was a member of the fitness center.

She had been in the bathroom changing her clothes when the employees closed the business and locked all the doors, locking her inside.

She was very upset. The woman said she was claustrophobic and was ready to break a window.

(That's not going to look good on that fitness employee's eval . . .)

A guy signed up to go on a police ride-a-long.

It is police procedure to do a background check on all persons before they go on the ride-a-long.

Subsequently, they found he had an outstanding warrant, and officers had to arrest him when he showed up.

Unfortunately, this was not the first time this has happened. If you think you might have an outstanding warrant, check before applying for that ride-a-long request so you can take care of the warrant first.

A hysterical woman ran to a neighbor's house and called 911.

She said she just arrived home from the grocery store.

When she walked into her bedroom, she found a large bump in her bed, under the covers.

She went on to say, her husband was out of town and no one should be in the house.

Officers rushed over . . . turns out it was a body pillow . . . .

We get many 911 calls from homes, businesses and payphones when no one is talking into the phone, but the line is open on the other end.

We refer to this as an 'open line.'

Sometimes, the caller accidentally dials. Sometimes there is an actual emergency. But for whatever reason, the caller is not able to say anything to the dispatcher.

Our policy is to stay on the line until a unit responds to evaluate the call.

On one occasion, one of our newer female dispatchers received a 911 call from a residence. It was an open line.

In keeping with the policy, she remained on the line, listening for any sign of an emergency or problem.

She soon realized that the phone must have been knocked off the hook by mistake.

The phone was in a couple's bedroom. The couple, who was obviously having sex, had not realized the phone accidentally called 911.

Officers did get out there and the dispatcher was able to disconnect.

(I guess that can be considered a 'right of passage' for our new dispatcher.)

(Oh and, by the way, all calls are recorded.)

—⟋⟍⟋—

A hit and run driver took off, but left the cops a nice present at the scene of the crime.

The suspect's license plate fell off his car on impact and was laying in the street.

—⟋⟍⟋—

A woman called in, complaining that a house or car alarm had been going off every 2-3 minutes for the past hour.

When officers got out there, the embarrassed caller realized it was her own car alarm that had been going off.

She promised to reset the alarm.

A 7.0 earthquake hit the Joshua Tree area. Later that day, we received a call from a woman accusing her boyfriend of moving their bed.

It wasn't the boyfriend, it was the earthquake.

A hysterical male called 911, screaming that he had been stabbed.

While officers and paramedics rushed out there, he suddenly realized he had been dreaming.

We cancelled the call, and hung up so the caller could go back to sleep.

A woman inside the fence of a public school asked a bystander outside the school to call police.

The embarrassed woman explained that she went in to the school to use the bathroom.

In the meantime, the gates to the school were locked by school staff, and she could not get out.

A woman called to report a large black bag in the back of a green station wagon parked at the end of the alley.

She thought it looked like a body could be inside the bag.

When officers got out there, they found a surfboard, not a body in the bag.

We received a 911 call from a payphone. It was an 'open line', with no one talking into the receiver.

The dispatcher could hear screaming in the background. The address is automatically generated on the screen and officers rushed over.

It turns out a security guard was showing his girlfriend how to use mace.

He accidentally sprayed his girlfriend and himself in the face with the mace.

They were at a water fountain washing out their eyes when police pulled up.

(The dispatcher joked to the responding officer, I hope that guy doesn't apply here at the police department, that mace could have been a gun!!)

Dispatcher: 911, what is your emergency?

Hysterical mother: I'm driving on the freeway.

My daughter fell out of the car somewhere on the freeway.

I turned around to look in the backseat and she wasn't there.

I had her strapped in her car seat. I don't know where she fell out.

The mother was hysterical, and the dispatcher scrambled to get the Highway Patrol checking the freeway also.

The thought of a child in her car seat, lying on the freeway had us all holding our breath . . .

San Diego Police officers and California Highway Patrol officers were all frantically looking for this baby.

Officers were searching for about 15 minutes . . . .

Suddenly, the distraught woman said, "Wait a minute, maybe I didn't pick her up from the babysitter."

Sure enough, the woman had had a temporary lapse of memory, and had thought she had already picked up her daughter, when she actually had not yet picked her up.

She drove to the sitter's place, and the child was still there, healthy and happy.

All's well that ends well . . . .

———∿———

Dispatcher   San Diego Police, how can I help you?

Embarrassed woman My friend and I are handcuffed to each other.

The key to the handcuffs broke off.

Can you please send the cops to get us out of these things?

———∿———

Dispatcher   911, what is your emergency?

Caller   I need paramedics. I was on my computer and suddenly became blind.

It turns out there was a power outage at his house and all the lights went out.

———∿———

We got a call of a man lying face down on the street.

The witness described him as wearing a black and white coat.

When officers and paramedics got out there, it turned out to be a large stuffed panda bear, not a man in the street.

CHAPTER EIGHTEEN

THE DARK SIDE

A word of warning . . . . If you want to read only the light hearted calls in this book, and finish the book with a smile, then skip this chapter.

However, I should also show the other side of our calls.

The reality is, most citizens calling 911 are in their darkest hour and are reaching out for help.

Along with the light hearted, interesting calls, there is a very sad, ugly, depressing side of the calls that come into the Communications Division on a daily basis.

Some calls are so sad, so heart wrenching that they will always stay with me. There are debriefings after a dispatcher gets a particularly difficult call.

But we are human. It can take its toll if you don't mentally leave the call at work when your shift is over.

Every moment, of every day, someone is being subjected to the ugliness of abuse, neglect, depression, violence and sadness.

Every night when I got home from work, I would hug my kids and thank God for the blessings in my life.

No matter how bad you think you have it, there is someone that is having a worse day.

No matter how little you think you have, there is someone that has less.

No matter how many afflictions you might have, there is someone that is worse.

So hug your kids a little tighter.

Tell those you love how much you love them, you never know if you will get another chance.

And be thankful for what you have.

Here are some examples of those calls.

Officers on a suicide call learned what led up to the suicide . . .

The victim had rear ended someone with his car.

He walked up to the other vehicle and asked the driver if they could settle this between themselves because he did not have insurance.

The other driver said 'no'.

The distraught victim then walked down an embankment and shot himself.

~~~~〰~~~~

Dispatcher: 911 what is your emergency?

Hospice Nurse: I have a 3 yr old female with cancer, having a hard time breathing . . .

~~~~〰~~~~

Dispatcher: San Diego 911, what is your emergency?

Calm caller: I need paramedics; I just got shot in the head with an arrow.

The caller was so calm, the dispatcher wasn't sure if he was joking around or was really shot in the head. But nonetheless, she got officers and paramedics started.

This was handled as a 'hot call', with the lead dispatcher on the line to help get information to everyone as quickly as possible.

The victim had been asleep in his apartment. He woke up feeling extreme pain in his head.

He looked in the mirror and saw the arrow in his head. It had entered from the back and almost went through his head by his eye cavity.

His roommate had deliberately shot him while he slept, and was going loading another arrow to shoot him again.

With the arrow still in his head, he managed to struggle with his roommate, then run to a neighbor's for help.

He was rushed to the hospital in critical condition. But he did survive that vicious, gruesome attack.

His roommate was arrested.

The dispatcher was at amazed how calm he was during the call. Maybe he was in shock. I don't know how many of us would have been that calm with an arrow through our head.

A woman called to report her 11 year old son missing for two days.

At one point during the call, the dispatcher put the caller on hold, muting the call.

The dispatcher was still able to hear the caller.

At that moment, the caller and her friend saw a man walk by.

The dispatcher heard the mother yell at the passerby, "You have a nice rear, come over here and I will give you some **business**."

I received a frantic call from a 16 year old student.

He lived in a rough neighborhood.

He was walking home from school, with no gang affiliation, minding his own business.

A group of gang bangers started harassing him, and demanding he tell them what gang he claims to be with.

He tried to tell them he was not with any gang. They pointed a gun at him and threatened to shoot him.

He ran and hid by a house.

Then he asked the resident if they could call the police for him. He came to the phone, and was so frightened, you could hear the panic in his voice.

It made me hurt for him, and all the young guys and girls who live in these neighborhoods where gangs have taken over.

Kids minding their own business, who can't walk down the street without being hassled, threatened or beaten up.

The only thing these young people are guilty of is living in a neighborhood that has been taken over by gangs.

Gangs that seem to think they own the streets. Everyone lives in fear.

If their parents are not financially able to move away from the area, these kids are stuck, and vulnerable.

Even walking to school puts them in harms way.

It's just heartbreaking.

—————〜〜〜—————

My heart skipped a beat any time I took a call of a car stuck on the railroad tracks.

Every second counts. I know there is a train moving down the tracks at a good rate of speed. But I don't know where it is, how far the train is from the car, and if I can get a hold of the railway dispatch center in time to stop it.

It felt like a race against time.

Getting the exact location of where the car was stuck, posed the first problem. It was usually difficult to pinpoint. Often the caller was not sure exactly where they were. And there were usually no street signs nearby.

Then, I had to determine if they were even in San Diego City's jurisdiction.

Next, having to determine which railroad train was involved . . . . Amtrak? Burlington?

Finally, I had to call that dispatch center to advise them of the hazard.

Hopefully all in time for them to stop the train.

Fortunately, I never had a bad outcome on the calls I took, but it sure raised my stress level.

One night I received a call from a 30 year old woman.

She was very distraught, and said she was going to kill herself. She had a loaded shotgun next to her.

I talked to her while officers rushed over to her apartment.

She told me she had a 5 year old daughter.

I tried to let her know how much her daughter must love her; how her daughter needs her, and would miss her mother if she did this.

I told her I could not imagine how she must be feeling. But I do know that things can get better.

She told me, she was having custody issues with the child's father. And felt hopeless because of financial problems.

I tried everything I could to get her to understand that there is help and hope out there. Nothing seemed to phase her.

As the officers pulled up outside her apartment . . . the woman abruptly hung up.

I had hoped she changed her mind, and put the gun away.

Unfortunately, after she hung up, she shot herself with the shotgun.

The officers that were there had to deal with the aftermath. We were all feeling the sadness, for her and her baby girl.

One of the officers sent me a message, asking how I was doing.

He told me nothing I could have said would have changed her mind. That did make me feel better, but I still wondered if there was something I could have said to make a difference.

Fortunately, her daughter was not home at the time, she spared her daughter that.

We receive suicide calls every day. Usually they call 911 because they are reaching out for help, and really don't want to follow through with killing themselves.

But this time, she was determined.

———〰〰———

A man called in to report two males tampering with a vehicle, either to steal or break into it.

#1 suspect was an adult male, #2 suspect appeared to be about 12 years old.

The caller said it looks like the adult could be the father of the younger suspect.

———〰〰———

We received a call from a father that reported his teenage son had poured rubbing alcohol in his water.

His son had a history of psychiatric problems.

The father went to the hospital.

Officers located his son and transported him to a psychiatric facility.

———〰〰———

An elderly woman with cancer was admitted to the hospital.

She was treated and improved enough to be released from the hospital.

When she walked into her house, she discovered everything inside was gone.

Evidently, her two selfish sons thought she was going to die and not return from the hospital.

It took no time for them to take everything she had.

All she had left was her hospital gown.

—〰—

Dispatcher: 911, what is your emergency?

Caller   My neighbor is stealing from me, he spikes my food, and when I pass out, he has sex with me.

Officers went out to evaluate the call.

—〰—

A concerned citizen called in to report her female neighbor left her 2 year old son alone while she went out to buy drugs.

The mother left about 11:00 p.m., and it was now about 3 o'clock in the morning.

The citizen could see the child running around the apartment.

Officers responded and found two young children alone; one child was in a full body cast from having two broken legs.

The children were removed from the apartment and transported for medical attention and safety.

———〰———

A man got into an argument with another man and hit him over the head with a 20 pound frozen tuna.

The victim sustained brain damage.

The suspect was arrested and charged with 'Assault with a Deadly Weapon'.

———〰———

A woman who was vacationing in Las Vegas called to say her purse had been stolen in Vegas. She did report the theft to the Las Vegas Police Department.

However, the suspects who stole her purse just called her cell phone to say they were inside her house in San Diego.

They described items in her house.

The suspects also said they killed her cat and made sexual threats to her.

To make matters even worse, the woman was very concerned because her two female roommates would be getting home from work shortly.

Officers rushed over. The suspects were no longer there.

They could not locate the cat.

But at least the officers got out there before the roommates got home.

—⁓⁓⁓—

A four year old was complaining that his foot hurt.

The caller checked, and found a small baggie of white substance tied around his toe.

His parents were subsequently arrested for drugs.

—⁓⁓⁓—

A 20 year old woman called 911 asking for poison control.

She purposely ingested about 15 seconds of raid in an attempt to kill herself.

She said she has strong periods of panic attacks which makes her want to end her life.

Officers responded and transported her to the hospital.

———ɯ̃———

Dispatcher   San Diego 911, what is your emergency?

Caller   My 16 year old son is totally out of hand. I don't know what to do.

             He is on probation, and a member of a very violent local gang.

             He just attacked me with a hot clothes iron and stole money out of my purse.

———ɯ̃———

A frantic woman flagged down a police car and said her husband kidnapped their 2 year old baby.

He told her he wants $3,000 for the safe return of the child.

The suspect made threats to sodomize the child and kill him if the money isn't brought to him.

———ɯ̃———

A woman called 911 saying she just shot her husband because he took away her cigarettes and wouldn't let her smoke.

When cops got there, she was still shooting him.

He died of multiple gunshot wounds.

Two suspects came up behind the caller.

They not only took his wallet with $200, and his radio, but they took the shoes off his feet.

The victim called us from a gas station.

It was late at night, and he was very cold.

It took him 2 hours to call police because he was so frightened.

I received a call from a 17 year old boy.

He had been staying in a very cheap motel with his mother and young sister.

He said he woke up to find his mother and little sister gone.

The mother had abandoned him.

The only thing she left with him was his birth certificate.

I always thought of gang members as mean, ruthless people, with no heart, and no soul.

I saw another side of them one night on my shift.

I took the 911 call around midnight.

It was a drive-by shooting and one of the members of a well known, hard core gang was shot.

I was on the line with one of the gang members while officers rushed over.

I was trying to get information on the suspect or suspect vehicle to give to the officers responding.

I could sense the pain in his voice as he held his friend who was dying in his arms.

His friend was bleeding and he knew he wasn't going to make it.

I was hearing a hard core gang member crying, pleading with his friend to 'hang in there'.

At that moment, I realized we may have taken different paths in life, but we all still have the ability to care, to love, and to show compassion.

I received this call on Mother's Day.

The mother calling 911 was so hysterical that it took me about 10 seconds to understand what she was saying.

She had just arrived home from church and found her 16 year old hanging from the doorway.

Police and paramedics rushed over.

The family frantically took him down and tried reviving him. During the mother's screams and panic, we could hear gurgling sounds.

We were hoping this was a good sign, and he would make it.

Unfortunately, he died.

He committed suicide.

That was one of the hardest calls for me. I will never forget it, and it often haunts me. Especially because my son was about the same age at the time.

How very sad for that poor mother, and family.

And how sad to think that he felt so hopeless, that death was his only solution.

CHAPTER NINETEEN

TRAINING TAPES

911 Police Dispatchers normally had eight weeks of training. The first two weeks was in an educational classroom setting. The trainer went through many different areas that we need to be proficient in before we start taking actual calls.

On our 3rd day of training, the trainer played several recorded tapes from actual calls taken in our Communications Center. All calls that come into the Comm Center are recorded.

Two of the calls made a tremendous impact on me. It was intended to serve as a lesson on what "Not" to do during a call.

The calls were very disturbing. It made me a better dispatcher than I might have been if I had not heard those two calls.

Here are the two tape recordings our trainer played for all new dispatcher trainees.

~~~~~∿∿~~~~~

It is Communication's policy to get the caller's address as soon as possible. It is one of the most important pieces of information needed for each call. This is one reason why.

Tape one:

A dispatcher received a 911 call from an elderly woman who lived alone.

The very first thing the woman did was start to give her address to the dispatcher.

Instead of letting the woman give her address, the dispatcher abruptly interrupted her and asked her why she was calling.

The woman then started to say a suspicious man was knocking on her neighbor's door.

All of a sudden the poor woman began screaming the most chilling screams I have ever heard.

The man had climbed in her window and was stabbing her to death.

She dropped the phone, but the line was still open, and her blood curdling screams continued. I will never forget those terrifying screams that seemed to go on forever. Knowing this woman was being stabbed, and dying.

To make a terrible situation even more devastating is the officers could not respond out there because they did not know where to go.

The dispatcher had interrupted the woman as she tried to give her address at the beginning of the call.

The woman had called us on the non-emergency line which does not display her address on the screen like it does when you call 911.

We were able to trace the call and eventually get officers out there.

The poor woman was dead, and the suspect was gone.

Chances are, even if we had her address, it would not have saved her life.

But it touched everyone sitting in that classroom. Everyone was silent for several minutes after the tape was over. We couldn't believe what we just heard.

I will never forget that call, and I never interrupted a caller giving their address because of it.

Tape two:

A man called 911 to say he just killed his wife with a hatchet.

The dispatcher had the address displayed and started officers out there.

She kept him on the line, both to make sure he doesn't leave, and to try and get more information.

He was describing what he did, and talked without emotion, and without remorse.

The dispatcher then asked the husband if she was still breathing.

The man then calmly said, "I don't know, let me check."

On the tape you can hear him drop the phone and walk over to his injured wife.

Then, you could hear him groan three times as he struck her with three more powerful blows with the hatchet.

After a minute, he came back to the phone.

He sounded out of breath.

Without emotion he told the dispatcher, that she was still breathing so he finished her off.

Officers got there and arrested him, but unfortunately they were not able to save the woman.

That tape made me realize just how important every question we ask is, and how a seemingly innocent question can set someone in a fragile or homicidal state, into a tailspin with drastic results.

———✿———

(I am glad I went with my intuition on this call)

There are two positions in Communications for assisting officers with searches, callbacks to reporting persons or anything the officers might need.

We rotate that position each night.

One particular night I was assigned this position.

It was about 3:00 in the morning.

An officer came upon a car stopped in the middle of an intersection.

No one was in the car. He assumed the car might be stolen and ran the license plate. The plate came back not stolen.

However, often a car taken during the night might not be reported stolen until the owner wakes up in the morning and discovers it missing.

So the officer asked me to try and find the phone number to the registered owner and see if they knew where their car was.

This is a fairly routine procedure.

I was able to find a phone number to the registered owner. So I made the call.

I let it ring several times, but got no answer.

Normally after 4 or 5 rings, we just hang up or leave a message on the answering machine. The officer will then just impound the vehicle until we hear from the owner.

But this particular time, something told me not to hang up. I felt like I needed to let it ring. I let it ring about 25 or 30 times.

Finally, an elderly woman answered.

Woman: Hello?

Dispatcher: Hello, this is dispatcher #160 from the San Diego Police Department, we located . . . .

Woman: Hello?

Dispatcher: Are you Mrs . . . .

Woman: I don't know . . .

It sounded like I woke the woman up, and she sounded confused and incoherent. I continued . . . .

Dispatcher: Are you okay ma'am?

Woman: I don't know . . .

I wasn't sure if she was just sleepy from being woke up or having a problem.

So I typed up a call for officers to go by the woman's house and check on her.

When officers got there, they found her on the floor, bleeding from stab wounds.

She was still breathing. Paramedics rushed her to the hospital.

But unfortunately, she didn't make it; she had been stabbed to death.

I was saddened that she did not survive.

But I was so glad I went with my instincts, not procedure and let the phone continue to ring. At least we gave her a fighting chance.

I felt so bad that I was the last one to hear her voice. That she didn't get a chance to say goodbye to those she loved.

I was saddened that this poor elderly woman, who was minding her own business, was killed by a stranger, in her home where she should have felt safe.

As it turned out, she was the first victim of a serial killer who targeted elderly women who lived alone in a section of our city.

He was eventually arrested.

One day a woman called because her boyfriend had made threats to kill himself.

He had taken his car and she had no idea where he was. He did have his cell phone with him. Fortunately, his phone was on.

I contacted his cell phone company to get the latitude and longitude co-ordinates of his cell phone. I obtained that and with more searches, zeroed in on the closest cell phone tower to his location.

This was still a large radius, and time was imperative. So I did some computer searches and found an address of a friend associated with him that lived in that area.

Officers went to that address, and he was there. He was okay, and they got him the help he needed.

When I was a new trainee, I was pretty nervous. I had not worked in an assignment where I had to make important split second decisions. I transferred from the Homicide Unit where the need for speed was not critical.

I had two wonderful trainers who gave me encouragement and kept me calm when it felt like my heart was going to pop out of my chest.

The call I was dreading most when I first started was my first "hot call", which is a 'crime in progress' call.

I think everyone worries about it. Until that right of passage happens, you wait for it.

Then it came . . . . My first hot call was a burglary in progress.

The caller said she saw two guys walking out of her neighbor's house carrying a shotgun and a lot of items out of the house. They jumped in a car and took off.

The man and woman who live there is an older couple, and were out of town at the time.

The caller had never seen that guy at their house before.

With the enhanced 911 system, the caller's address is normally displayed on the screen.

When I saw her address, I immediately recognized the street as my cross street.

The house being burglarized was my neighbor's house at the end of my block.

The fact that this was my very first 'hot call' and it happened to be my neighbor made the adrenaline flow even faster.

But I got through it, and because of the alertness of the witness, the police were able to locate the suspects within 20 minutes of the call.

CHAPTER TWENTY

PAY IT FOWARD

One day, a Vietnam Veteran called 911, very distraught and having thoughts of committing suicide.

I told him we would get officers out there to help him.

While we waited for the officers to get there, I stayed on the line with him and we talked.

He expressed his disappointment with the system.

He said he was proud to serve our country, but then when he needed help, no one seemed to care and he could not get any help.

He was homeless and had no family in San Diego.

He had no job here. There was a job waiting for him in Oregon, but he had no money to get up there.

He was not asking for a hand out. He was not asking for something for nothing.

He just wanted to know that our country cared. And it sounded like he was let down.

Officers got on scene, and transported him to the County Mental Health (C.M.H.) facility, where he was placed on a voluntary 72 hour hold.

I felt so bad for this veteran who had served our country, and was willing to lay down his life for our freedom, and then felt like his country turned its back on him when he needed help.

So when I was done with my shift, I went to the bus station and bought him a one-way ticket to Oregon.

I went to C.M.H. where I left the bus ticket with the receptionist.

I asked that she give him the ticket along with a note I wrote, thanking him for his service, and to let him know people do care.

A few weeks later, he sent a postcard to Communications, thanking me and the officers who had transported him to C.M.H.

He said he was doing well in Oregon.

I hope he is still doing well.

It was the early morning hour, about 3:00 am when I took a call from a Vietnam Veteran suffering from Post Traumatic Stress Disorder.

He ran out of his medication. He couldn't get his prescription filled until morning.

He did not want to go to the hospital; he just needed someone to talk to. We were not busy at that time of the morning . . . So I was able to just talk to him, until he felt better.

My heart went out to him. He was calling from a low rent hotel in downtown San Diego.

I thought of how his life might have been different if he hadn't suffered the emotional pain of being in that ugly war.

My kids and I were going to Washington D.C. the next week. I promised to get something for him when I returned. We did do what I had promised, but I misplaced his address, and still have the items. If he happens to read this, please contact the publisher and I will get those things to you.

MY TWO CENTS

God Bless our men and women in the military, past, present and future.

No one can ever really understand the horrors and pain they have endured protecting our freedom.

I know I can never understand the full scope of what they have been through.

Each and every business in America that enjoys free enterprise and the freedom for opportunity should thank a Vet.

I urge everyone to do their part. It starts with each of us.

When you are in line for coffee and a military man or woman is in line, buy them a cup of coffee.

If you are in line at the grocery store, pay for part of their groceries.

If you see them eating at a restaurant, pay their bill.

Or just go up to them, shake their hand, and thank them for their bravery, and for their service.

It will make you feel good, and it will show them how much we appreciate their sacrifice and what they do for us.

My best Christmas ever was the year my son and I really felt the Christmas Spirit. It was the best feeling ever, and that I will never forget.

It was close to Christmas when I received a call from a caring mother who had an 8 year old son. Her husband, a veteran, had recently died.

They were living in a motel, and she had no money to buy her son a present.

So she called Communications to see if she could sign up for one of the charities that were giving gift donations.

I was fortunate to have gotten the call.

I knew it was too close to Christmas. I knew the charities had been depleted of gifts and giving her phone numbers to try would have been fruitless.

So I got her phone number and asked if I could call her after my shift was over.

I asked her what her son wanted, and she told me he had asked for a football.

When I got home, I told my son, Mike, about the call. He wanted to help too.

So we went to Toys R Us and bought a football. While we were there, we decided to get a couple more things for him. So we bought a different kind of football, a razor scooter, (which was the hot toy that year), and made up a stocking with candy.

The next day, Mike and I went to the motel and delivered the gifts to the mother and son.

The look on the young boy's face when he saw the gifts was something I will never forget.

He was so very happy.

When he opened the second football, he said, "Look mama, I must have been very very good . . . Santa gave me **two** footballs!"

When he opened the scooter, he started jumping up and down.

The young boy was so polite, and sweet.

His mother was also very appreciative. She said she never expected anything like that.

They both thanked us many times.

Mike and I walked away feeling on top of the world.

The saying, "It is better to give than to receive", was never clearer then at that moment.

At the time, my son was working at Albertsons, a major grocery store. He had been working in the Christmas tree lot of the store. There were still many trees that had not been sold.

So Mike took his pitch up with management and persuaded the store to donate most of the remainder of the trees.

I then called the Salvation Army for a list of working families that were struggling, and could not afford to buy a Christmas tree.

They notified 38 families and asked if it would be okay to give us their addresses so we could deliver the trees.

Then Mike got several of his friends who had pickups. We loaded up the trees in the trucks.

Then convoyed to each house, delivering the trees. It was so much fun. We loved every minute of it.

What a wonderful feeling it gave each of us.

We delivered one tree to an apartment where a 3 year old boy lived with his mother. She too could not afford to buy him a present.

So we returned the next day with a present for him.

When we walked into the apartment, we saw the tree in the living room. It had only four candy canes on it for decorations.

As we were about to leave, the boy gave us a hug, then ran to the tree, took one of the candy canes and ran back over to us.

He proudly reached out his hand to give it to us. It was so sweet.

CHAPTER TWENTY-ONE

LETTERS FROM CHILDREN

Every day, we receive 911 calls from children who call 911 when there is no emergency.

Some call out of curiosity because they are taught in school to call if there is a problem.

Many times, a parent will call 911 with the child to teach them how to reach help if they ever need it.

For these reasons, dispatchers and police officers are very understanding.

Parents are actually encouraged to teach their kids how and when to call 911.

We never want to scold a child who is curious or calls because they are scared for whatever reason. This might cause them to hesitate calling if they ever do have an emergency.

There are also some kids who call 911 because they are mischievous or bored. We want these bored kids to realize that when they call 911 for fun, it is tying up the lines for people who are having real emergencies.

The following letters are from children who had called 911 for fun.

I would like to express my thanks and respect to the parents of these children for teaching them the right thing to do.

And to thank the children for writing the letters.

Dear Poilce and fire department · I am really
Sorry that I called nine one one when it
wasn't an emegancy I learned that you don't
call nine one one when it is not an emergancy
you call incase it's an emergancy. my great
great grampa and uncle were fire fighters I'm
really sorry I promouse that I will never
do this again

love

Tyler

11-27-07

Dear 911 Police Dispatchers,

You're the best! The knocking on the door thing was a brilliant idea. You have an important job. If it wasn't for you guys we wouldn't have a good community. When I grow up I want to be just like you. You help catch burgalars and help save the day. I like the way you protect us from the bad guys. Thanks for your help!

Sincerly,
Eric

208

Dear San Diego Police Department,
I'm sorry for calling you. I won't
do it again. I am very disappointed in myself.
I'm so sorry for setting a real bad example
for my school. I will never call 911 again.
I promise I will not call it again. Unless I
have an emergency. I am so sorry,
I feel bad about doing what I did. I know
my teachers are disappointed because I called
you and I didn't have an emergency. I am
so sorry. I know I did bad for calling
you. I hope you can forgive me.

Sincerely,

Karen ▮▮▮▮▮

Dear 911 Emergency,   6-27-94
        I dialed 911 just to see what
would happen. It was wrong. I am very
very sary. Your job is very important
to people who realy need help. I will
never dialed 911 again inles it is an
emergency.

                        Sincerly,

                        Jessica ■
                        ━━━━━━━━━━━━━

                ━━━

211

2/14/00 David ███

Dear: San Diego Police Department,
I am sorry that I called 911 with ███
of that again. I did something wrong ██ I
I was not suppose to do. I'll you
forgive me for what I did? Next time
of ██ ██ a phone I will not pick
it up or even touch it again unless a
have good reason to. I won't cal
unless it is a real emergency. I will no
call just for fun. I was not a good re
presentative for my school. I was a bad
example.

                    Sincerely,
            David ███

212

Palis man

.I am so
Sory Wat happind
acupl days ugo.
no buty in
My Family will evr
coll 911 agin enles
.thars a red anir-
jensi.

From,

C ██████ J ██████
and T ██████

CHAPTER TWENTY-TWO

OFFICERS, DISPATCHERS EXPRESSIONS

Holidays and Super Bowl days are usually pretty slow in Communications, until the inebriated party goers start fighting. So during the slow down time, creative officers have shown their artistic side with the following done from their computers.

```
ntered    12/24/92   16:54:01
losed     12/25/92   13:31:17

nitial Type: 211CJ
inal    Type: 211CJ    (ROBBERY CAR JACKING)
olice BLK:
eat:
oc: BOL FOR 211/207 "SLEIGHJACKING" FROM NORTH POLE!

oc Info:
ame: NORTH POLE PD              Addr: 1 NORTH POLE LN        Phone: SANTACLAUS
```

. ALL UNITS B O L FOR 211 SLEIGHJACKING FROM NORT
H POLE, OCCURRED 122492 , UNK TIME ELEMENT. VICTI
M VEH DESCRIBED AS FULL SIZED SLEIGH WITH METAL R
UNNERS.
. VEH SHOULD BE PULLED BY EIGHT TINY REINDEER AND
 POSSIBLY LED BY AN ADDITIONAL REINDEER WITH A RE
D NOSE.
. VEHICLE SHOULD ALSO BE FULL OF TOYS IN LARGE BA
GS WHICH WERE INTENDED FOR MANY CHILDREN THROUGHO
UT THE WORLD.
. VICTIM OF 207 IS STILL IN THE SLEIGH DESCRIBED
AS A WMA "S. CLAUS", WMA UNK AGE, EXTREMELY HEAVY
 SET, WITH LONG WHI HAIR, LONG WHI BEARD AND MUST
ACHE, BUSHY RED CHEEKS.
. LAST SEEN WEARING A RED/WHI FURRY SUIT AND RED
CAP AND BLACK BOOTS..//
. POSSIBLE SUSP INVOLVED IN THIS IS A MALE WITH A
 LONG GRAY BEARD, EXTREMELY SKINNY, POSS NICKNAME
D "GRINCH". POSS SUSP ENRT TO "WHOVILLE", NFD.
. FOR INFO THIS VEHICLE IS ONLY ABLE TO TRAVEL FR
OM ROOFTOP TO ROOFTOP SO UNITS SHOULD PAY SPECIAL
 ATTENTION TO THOSE AREAS...//
. ANY INFO FOR NORTH POLE P D REF CASE #122492...
STATION A...//
. 19:26:02 TO RADIO FROM   I THINK WE JUST S
AW THE SLAY AT 700 E SAN YSIDRO....'.
. 20:17:41 TO RC05 FROM   I THINK I SPOTTED T
HAT 10851 SLEIGH....IT WAS WEST BOUND AT ABOUT 25
00 FEET....YOU MIGHT TRY LINDBERG FIELD TO SEE IF
 THEY PICKED IT UP ON RADAR....IT WAS GETTING RID
 OF EVIDENCE BY THROWING WRAPPED PACKAGES OUT OVE
R SOUTHERN SAN DIEGO

215

GGED DOWN AT 3000 CORONADO REF THE SLEIGHJACKER V
EH...LAST SEEN BY THE YOUNG LOVERS UP HERE PKED O
N A ROOFTOP TO THE SOUTH...UNK STREET. THE LISTED
 SUS DROPPED DOWN A CHIMNEY CARRYING BAGS MARKED
"COAL". HE THEN ROSE OUT OF THE CHIMNEY AND SAW T
HEM WATCHING. HE BLACKED OUT THE RAINDEERS NOSE A
ND TOOK OFF AT A HIGH R.O.S. W/B AT AB
,OUT 12,000 FEET. BE CKING THE AREA
, 05:50:28   :I JUST SAW THAT SL
EIGH WIZ PAST MY H IN CREST BOY IT WAS HAULING I
DIDNT KNOW IT WAS A 10851 OR I WOULD HAVE SENT CL
IFF THE WONDER THE DOG AFTER THE SKINNY DRIVER

216

```
 SSS   U   U  PPP   EEEEE  RRR
S   S  U   U  P   P E      R   R
 S     U   U  PPP   EEEE   RRR
S   S  U   U  P     E      R   R
 SSS    UUU   P     EEEEE  R   R

       BBB   OOO   W     W  L
       B  B  O   O W     W  L
       BBB   O   O W  W  W  L
       B  B  O   O W W W W  L
       BBB   OOO    W   W   LLLLL

       BBB   OOO   U   U  N   N  DDD     !!!!!!!!
       B  B  O   O U   U  NN  N  D   D    !!!!!!
       BBB   O   O U   U  N N N  D   D      !!!
       B  B  O   O U   U  N  NN  D   D
       BBB   OOO    UUU   N   N  DDD         !
```

217

```
01/28/96  08:33:35 PRINT REQUESTED BY TERMINAL ████
01/28/96  06:13:24 TO COMM FROM ████:
FROM ANOTHER FOOTBALL FAN:)
01/28/96  06:13:01 TO ██ FROM ████

01/28/96  06:12:04 TO ████ FROM
████.


XXXXXXXXXXXXXXXXXXXXXXXXXXXXXXXXXXX
XXXXXXXXXXXXXXXXXXXXXXXXXXXXXXXXXXX
XXXXX     XXXXXXXXXXXXXXXXXXXXXXXXX
XXX       XXXXXXXXXXXXXXXXXXXXXXXX
XX    /\     XXXXXX    SUPERBOWL    XX
X    ' .     XXXXXX     CHAMPS      XX
X    \/    XXXXXXX    PITTSBURG    XX
X          XXXXXXXX   STEELERS!    XX
XX             XXXXXXXXXXXXXXXXXXXXX
XXX    O    XXXXXXXXXXXXXXXXXXXXXXXX
XXXXX       XXXXXXXXXXXXXXXXXXXXXXXX
XXXXXXXXXXXXXXXXXXXXXXXXXXXXXXXXXXXX
XXXXXXXXXXXXXXXXXXXXXXXXXXXXXXXXXXXX
```

```
01/29/95  15:29:39 PRINT REQUESTED BY TERMINAL ████
01/29/95  14:46:59 TO ████  FROM ████:

01/29/95  14:30:13 TO ████  FROM ████
```

GO

CHARGERS !!!

```
12/25/95  15:11:06 PRINT REQUESTED BY TERMINAL ████
12/25/95  15:10:14 TO ████ FROM ████:

12/25/95  15:09:50 TO ████ FROM ████

12/25/95  15:09:07 TO ██ FROM ████
TWAS THE AFTERNOON OF CRISTMAS AND ALL THRU THE BEAT.NOT A CREATURE WAS STIRRING
.ONLY US HEAT. OUR MDT'S WERE PARKED AT 10-8 WITH CARE.IN HOPE THAT NO CALLS WOU
LD SHOW UP ON THERE.  WE SAY THAT TONIGHT THERE WILL BE NO FIGHT.TO ALL MY FELLO
W COPPERS I WISH A GOOD NIGHT!!!!
```

```
12/17/94   20:09:25 PRINT REQUESTED BY TERMINAL CT06
12/17/94   20:09:04 TO COMM FROM CT20:
FOR YOU WHO JST ARRIVED..............
THIS WAS SAVED..KINDA CUTE.

12/16/94   23:46:31 TO RADIO FROM RC05:


FROM 611J3/

.       _  _
.       _  -\\              /|
.     /|\     (")           \_\
.     \/\[] /#\..................... /.\
.     \_[[]ᴸ__)    __               __
.      |        |))   | |       .'       /
.      |     \2__/   |  \       \        |
.      |_____|   ))     ( /---\ /
.        ||        ||  //       \\\    ||
.      *...............*/        -     **
.
.
.
.
```

**** MERRY CHRISTMAS AND HAPPY NEW YEAR ****

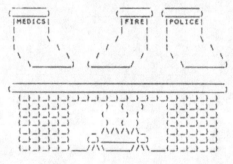

222

```
12/25/95  15:15:00 PRINT REQUESTED BY TERMINAL CT29
12/25/95  15:14:56 TO COMM FROM RS01:


12/25/95  15:14:34 TO MOTS FROM 625J1:

12/25/95  08:06:43 TO 625J1 FROM
625J1:


XXXXXXXXXXXXXXXXXXXXXXXXXXXXXXXXXXXXXXXX
XXXX      XXXX HAPPY     XXXXXXXXXXXXXXXX
XXX X _____XXX HOLIDAYS XX XXXXXXXXXXXX
XX   XX  .XXXXXXXXXXXXXX XXXXXXXXXXXX
XXXXXX    _ XXXXXXXXXXXXXX .XXXXXXXXXX
XXXXXXX\  XXXXXXXXXXXXXXX   XXXXXXXX
XXXXXXX_____  | XXXXXXXXX  XXXXXXXXX
XX  XXX_____[]XX --0--0--0--0--0--X
XX        XX XXX         XXXXX      X
XX             X  XX XXXXXX XXXXX XXX
XXX XXXXXXXX XX  XX  XXXXXX  XX   XXX
X              XXXXXXXXXXXXXXXXXXXXX
XXXXXXXXXXXXXXXXXXXXXXXXXXXXXXXXXXXXXX
```

223

```
01/01/95  05:00:37 PRINT REQUESTED BY TERMINAL CT09
01/01/95  00:23:20 TO COMM FROM RS01:

01/01/95  00:22:15 TO 2927N3 FROM
2927N3:
BOOMER WISHES YOU A HAPPY
```

CHAPTER TWENTY-THREE

INSIDE COMMUNICATIONS

I loved working in Communications.

We were like a family, and the 19 years went by really fast.

I thought I would share a few funny stories.

―――₪₪₪―――

The next three stories demonstrate my weakness for chocolate.

Three stories I am not particularly proud of . . . . ☺

National Dispatcher Week is every April. Officers and others who have worked with us during the year will often bring goodies into the Communications Division.

My brother, Jim, is a San Diego Police Officer. He would usually bring a two pound box of yummy chocolates into Communications.

One year, he bought the box of candy, and asked me to bring it in for everyone to share.

Well, he should have known me.

I took the candy with very good intentions. But he gave it to me on Friday. I had to resist the temptation to open the box for three days.

I didn't make it.

By Monday, I had eaten the entire two pounds of chocolates.

Then the dilemma . . .

I could just keep silent, not tell the dispatchers he bought the candy and just hope they don't find out . . . .

But what if he asks them how they liked it?

I opted to do the right thing, own up to it and take the hit . . . .

So when I got to work that Monday, I reluctantly sent a computer message around to all the dispatchers on the shift that went something like this . . . .

> **"Good Morning my DEAREST friends . . .**
>
> **My brother Jim gave me a 2 pound box of Sees candy to give to all of you, but I ended up eating the entire box.**
>
> **I know I should be sorry . . . but I'm not . . ."**

Then, I waited for the fallout . . . .

Well, I heard a few laughs and a few gasps . . . . then the messages started firing back at me . . . .

I hope they go directly to your hips! . . .

You owe us a box of candy! . . .

Have you no shame! . . . .

How could you eat two pounds of chocolate in 3 days! . . .

Etc, etc, etc . . . .

Ten years later, they still remembered . . . . and joked about it.

Hey, when it comes to chocolate . . . I have no shame . . .

—————

Another day . . .

Someone brought in home made chocolate chip cookies.

I couldn't wait for my first break to go into our lunch room and get one.

I was three days into my diet, and should have resisted the cookies.

I was limiting myself to a very low daily calorie count. So eating a cookie would have put me over my limit.

Well, I ate one . . . and it was soo good. So I ended up eating three cookies.

My son, Mike was my diet coach. I called him on my next break and told him that I ate three chocolate chip cookies.

He said in a very disappointing voice . . . "Oh mom . . . . what were you thinking?!!"

I thought for a second and said,

"What was I thinking? . . . . I was thinking . . ." mmmmm free cookies . . . !!"

Another day,

During my shift . . . . A message went around the room to all dispatchers . . . .

A citizen who had called in for assistance last week wanted to thank all of you . . . Kudos for everyone . . .

Well, I got very excited, and couldn't wait for my next break to get my Kudo.

My break came, and I went into the lunchroom, but was very disappointed. There were no Kudos there.

When I got back from break, I asked where the Kudos were.

Well, how was I supposed to know that kudos was just a "thank you", and not the actual candy bars?

—⁓⋘⁓—

One Halloween, I didn't really want to dress up for work, but wanted to do something.

So I cut a 4 foot strip of a white sheet, the width of toilet paper. I took a pen and made marks like perforations. Then I stapled one end to an empty roll of toilet paper. I stuck the other end in the back waistband of my pants.

We all have line-up before each shift that everyone attends. This is to discuss any information that we need to know before our shift starts.

I waited until everyone was in line-up, and just before the supervisor started talking.

Then, with the toilet paper following behind me, I walked into line-up and walked across the room, and sat on the other side.

I said out loud . . . "Sorry I'm late; I had to go to the bathroom."

I could hear the muffled laughs, and surprised looks. It looked real. I acted like I didn't know what they were laughing at.

No one said anything until lineup was over.

Then I found out who my 'real' friends were, by who told me that I had toilet paper in my pants.

———~m~———

One of our best supervisors was an awesome free spirit named Charlene.

She had a great personality and had us in stitches whenever she gave line-up. (Departmental briefings with all dispatchers and a supervisor each day, before our shift.)

We got this next call soon after September 11th, 2001, when patriotism was rekindled and most everyone seemed to be touched with American pride.

Charlene was the supervisor working that day.

A woman called in complaining about the excessive jet noise at the Miramar Navy Base.

The dispatcher told the woman she would have to call the Navy Base and talk to them. The woman did not like that answer, got very irate and demanded to talk to a supervisor.

The dispatcher then transferred the woman to our supervisor, Charlene.

Charlene patiently waited while the woman complained about the terrible noise the jets make when they go by her house.

Well, you could almost hear the "Star Spangled Banner" playing in the background when Charlene said in a proud patriotic voice . . . .

"That's the sounds of freedom ma'am . . . . the sounds of freedom . . . !

I don't know what the woman said after that remark, but my guess is she was speechless . . .

———ɯɯ———

I enjoyed going to work, taking calls and being with friends.

Three friends in particular were very close to me. For almost twenty years, we celebrated with birthday lunches, went to the movies, and just hung out together.

One day, we went to the movies, and then had lunch at an Italian restaurant, called Buca Di Beppo.

It's a very interesting restaurant, with hundreds of old fashion family photos all over the walls.

We thought it would be fun to get one of our photos and add it to the wall.

So a few weeks later we went back to the restaurant. I took a photo of the 4 day cruise we recently went on, put Velcro on the back, and stuck it on one of the walls among all the other pictures.

As we were leaving, the waiter said, "Good bye ladies, see you later".

My friend said, "You'll see us first!"

He had a perplexed look on his face, and probably thought we were crazy.

We went back several times, and the photo was still there.

I wonder if they discovered it yet. I'll have to go back again and check.

Speaking of that cruise . . .

The four of us got a really good deal on a 4 day cruise to Mexico.

We had a great time for the first 3 days. The night before we were going home, disaster struck . . . .

We had just finished dinner and were rushing to get to the show.

We were walking down the stairs a little too fast when one of my friends slipped on the stairs and landed on her shoulder.

You should have seen how graceful she went down; it was almost in slow motion.

When she landed, I don't know what happened . . . seeing her gracefully going down, trumped our compassion, I guess.

Suddenly, the whole scenario became hysterically funny.

Poor Jeanne was still on the stairs, and the rest of us were laughing uncontrollably.

Shirley and I were trying to gain composure to help the poor girl up . . .

Carolyn started walking away, still laughing, with her legs crossed.

She said, "Sorry, I'd like to stay and help, but I can't, I'm peeing my pants."

Poor Jeannie, she really hurt her shoulder. I am sorry we laughed.

CHAPTER TWENTY FOUR

DEDICATION

I would like to dedicate this book to my wonderful father, Frank.

He was a World War II Veteran.

He was the greatest man I have ever known. I never once heard him raise his voice. He never swore, and never talked about anyone behind their back.

He was a very gentle, caring, decent man who never hurt anyone, but would do anything to protect his family.

He stood up for what he believed in.

The older I got, and the more people I encountered along the way, the more I appreciated how exceptional he was.

He was a very hard working man. For a time he was a milkman. This was when glass milk bottles were delivered to your house.

Sometimes he had customers that would not pay their bill. If there were children in the house, he would continue to deliver milk. He would see liquor bottles on the kitchen table. Even though he knew he would not get paid, he did not want to deprive the kids of milk.

I wish I could be like him. But I don't know how he went through life never yelling, never swearing, never gossiping and always doing the right thing.

He helped me strive for it, even though I could never come close to achieving it.

Thank you dad, for all the love, for rocking us kids to sleep every night until we were six years old.

I miss you. I know you are watching over me from Heaven, I hope this book makes you proud.

CHAPTER TWENTY FIVE

SPECIAL THANKS

I would like to thank God for all my blessings.

Next, I would like to thank my beautiful, sweet daughter, Maria, my very talented, caring son Mike, and my beautiful, sweet granddaughters, Brianna and Rachel.

I have cherished all the love, hugs, and wonderful memories each of you have given me since the day you were born. I love you.

I'd like to thank my fiancé, Richard for loving me so much. For being my rock, and always being there for me. I never thought I would find such a decent, wonderful man. I love you.

I would like to thank my mom, for all the years of helping me. For all the school lunches you packed for me. For all the clean clothes, the ironed clothes, the great dinners and P.T.A meetings you attended. I love you.

To Jim, Frank, Frankie, Erik and Jerrica, I love you.

Thank you all for being a wonderful part of my life.

Finally, I would like to thank dispatch trainers, Joann P., and Mike B.. They made a big difference during my training process. They gave me positive feedback that gave me confidence, patience that helped me stay calm, and the expertise that carried me through my 8 weeks of training, and my 19 years as a 911 Police Dispatcher.

It was a great 26 year career. I worked in Records, Homicide and Communications. I loved every minute of it. I miss the work, and the people I worked with.

Most of all, I miss the 911 calls. I loved being able to help people, and hopefully at times made a positive difference.

CHAPTER TWENTY SIX

SEMINARS AND CLASSES I ATTENDED

- Feb. 1985 Safety Training Certificate

- Aug. 1985 Supervisory Management

- Aug. 1985 Appointing Authority—Interview Training

- Sept. 1986 Supervisory Update—It's OK to be boss

- Nov . 1986 Post Assertive Supervision

- Feb. 1987 Constructive Confrontation

- Feb. 1988 Building Advanced Skill for Effective Performance

- Sept. 1988 POST Personnel Management

- Nov. 1992 Public Safety Dispatcher

- Nov. 1992 Complaint Dispatcher

- Mar. 1997 Diversity Training

- April 1998 How to deal with Employee Attitude Problems

- Dec. 1998 Telecommunications Information Gathering

- Sept. 2000 Public Safety Dispatcher

- Oct. 2000 Hate Crimes

- Mar. 2001 Suicide by Cop

- Jun. 2001 Domestic Violence & Hostage Negotiations

- Jul. 2001 Domestic Violence & Hostage Negotiations—Continued

- Aug. 2001 Missing Persons Overview

- Sept. 2001 Public Safety Dispatcher

- Jan. 2002 Domestic Violence

- Jan. 2001 Elder Abuse issues for Dispatchers

- March 2002 Late Life Domestic Violence

- Sept. 2002 Meeting the Ethical Challenge

- Nov. 2002 Becoming Culturally Competent

- Jun. 2003 Suicidal, Emotional Callers, critical Incident Review, advanced Stress Management for Dispatchers

- Sept. 2003 Stalking

- Dec. 2003 Hostage Negotiations

- Jun. 2004 Meeting the Professional Challenge

- Jun. 2004 Kids in Peril

- Jun. 2004 Recognizing Terrorism

- Jun. 2004 Hate Crimes

- Aug. 2004 Terrorism Awareness for Dispatchers

- Sept. 2004 Recognizing Mental Illness

- Dec. 2004 Crisis Communications

- Mar. 2005 Active Shooter 1st Responder

- Apr. 2005 Dispatcher Wellness

- Jun. 2005 Tools for The Trainer

- Apr. 2006 Terrorism Awareness

- Dec. 2006 Train the Trainer

- Jul. 2007 FEMA

- Sept. 2007 Hostage Negotiations

- Sept. 2007 Customer Service and Professionalism

- Aug. 2008 Field Tactics for Dispatchers

ABOUT THE AUTHOR

I was fortunate enough to have had a long and fruitful career at the San Diego Police Department that lasted 26 years. I worked in several units, but some of the most memorable moments stemmed from my 19 year stay in the Communications Division as a 911 dispatcher. My job was to be a voice on the other end of the phone to offer help no matter what the situation was.

Usually, the calls were serious and made me count the minutes until I went home and hugged my family, and other times the calls were down right hilarious.

One thing stayed constant . . . when I answered the phone as Dispatcher #160, I had to be prepared for anything. As a dispatcher, I had to quickly adapt from one call to the next. One call could be devastating where there was a death, and the very next call was an irate citizen yelling because their neighbor was having a loud party. Even though I was still emotionally affected by the last call, I had to keep in mind that this noise complaint was important to this caller. So I handled the noise complaint with the same professionalism and attentiveness as the previous death call.

I loved being a 911 dispatcher. To me, it was more than a job, it was a calling. It was very rewarding when I was able to help someone at their darkest hour. I cared about each call I took. It is for that reason that I am proud to have maintained a level of professionalism that I know matched a very high standard. I am blessed to have had the opportunity to make a positive impact on people's lives.

Determining how to handle each call, within seconds of receiving it, with so much on the line was more stressful then most could imagine. One way many dispatchers were able to handle this burden was to do as much as we could for those who needed our help, but also to enjoy and cherish the lighter moments that made this book possible.

I hope you enjoy reading this book as much as I enjoyed writing it.